CHARLES DICKENS

A BEGINNER'S GUIDE

ROB ABBOTT AND CHARLIE BELL

Series Editors
Rob Abbott & Charlie Bell
Drawings
Steve Coots

Hodder & Stoughton

A MEMBER OF THE HODDER HEADLINE GROUP

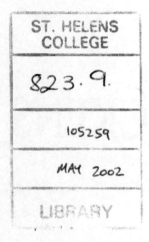
Orders: please contact Bookpoint Ltd, 130 Milton Park, Abingdon, Oxon OX14 4SB. Telephone: (44) 01235 827720, Fax: (44) 01235 400454. Lines are open from 9.00–6.00, Monday to Saturday, with a 24-hour message answering service. Email address: orders@bookpoint.co.uk

British Library Cataloguing in Publication Data
A catalogue record for this title is available from The British Library

ISBN 0 340 789018

First published 2001
Impression number   10 9 8 7 6 5 4 3 2
Year   2005 2004 2003 2002

Copyright © 2001 Rob Abbott and Charlie Bell

Artist Steve Coots
Typeset by Transet Limited, Coventry, England.
Printed in Great Britain for Hodder & Stoughton Educational, a division of Hodder Headline Plc, 338 Euston Road, London NW1 3BH by Cox & Wyman, Reading, Berks

CONTENTS

Contents

Introduction

HOW TO USE THIS BOOK

The *Beginner's Guide* series aims to introduce readers to the major writers of the past 500 years. It is assumed that readers will begin with little or no knowledge and will want to go on to explore the subject in other ways.

BEGIN READING THE AUTHOR

This book is a companion guide to Dickens' major works; it is not a substitute for reading the books themselves. It would be useful if you read one of Dickens' works in parallel, so that you can put theory into practice. This book is divided into chapters. After considering how to approach the author's work and a brief biography, we go on to explore some of Dickens' main writings and themes before examining some critical approaches to the author. The survey finishes with suggestions for further reading and possible areas of additional study.

HOW TO APPROACH UNFAMILIAR OR DIFFICULT TEXTS

Coming across a new writer may seem daunting, but do not be put off. The trick is to persevere. Much good writing is multi-layered and complex. It is precisely this diversity and complexity which makes literature rewarding and exhilarating.

Literature often needs to be read more than once, and in different ways. These ways can include: a leisurely and superficial reading to get the main ideas and narrative; a slower more detailed reading focusing on the nuances of the text, concentrating on what appear to be key passages; and reading in a random way, moving back and forth through the text to examine such things as themes, narrative or characterisation. Every reader has their own approach but undoubtedly the best way to extract the most from a text is to read it several times.

In complex texts it may be necessary to read in short chunks. Sometimes the only way to get by is to skip through the text, going back over it later. When it comes to tackling difficult words or concepts it is often enough to guess in context on the first reading, making a more detailed study using a dictionary or book of critical concepts on later reading. If you prefer to look up unusual words as you go along, be careful that you do not disrupt the flow of the text and your concentration.

VOCABULARY

You will see that **key terms** and unfamiliar words are set in **bold** text. These words are defined and explained in the GLOSSARY to be found at the back of the book. In order to help you further we have also included a **summary** of each chapter.

You can read this introductory guide in its entirety, or dip in wherever suits you. You can read it in any order. It is a tool to help you appreciate a key figure in literature. We hope you enjoy reading it and find it useful.

✷✷✷✷SUMMARY✷✷✷✷

To maximise the use of this book:

- Read the author's work.

- Read it severval times in different ways.

- Be open to innovative or unusual forms of writing.

- Persevere.

Rob Abbott and Charlie Bell
Series Editors

Why Read Dickens Today?

A POPULAR WRITER

Charles Dickens was a prolific writer. He was frequently writing more than one novel at a time in serial form for literary magazines, as well as editing the magazines himself and taking an enormous interest in the science, arts and politics of the day. Since he began writing his novels, he has remained popular with the reading public. He has also been a fascinatingly controversial figure, being by turns dismissed and then rehabilitated by literary academics; continuously reinterpreted by various theories and traditions in the literary world; serialised in the Sunday afternoon slot by the BBC in the 1960s; and now filmed and televised in various guises and adaptations.

But is he a good writer?

The very reasons that make him a popular writer also make him controversial. At the centre of this paradox lies the debate as to whether he is simply a populist writer creating a profusion of mind-boggling caricatures and untenable plots, or whether he can be considered a 'serious' author. In simple terms, is he a good writer or a bad one? The discussion takes many forms and over the last 150 years has reached many conclusions. It is the intention of this book to follow some of these debates, particularly those of modern academics, and to help you apply some of the theoretical views encapsulated within them to a number of the main works. We hope you will feel able to draw your own conclusions.

Character or caricature?

Let us begin with the characters themselves. Whatever aesthetic judgement we may draw, it is self-evident that Dickens' characters are at the heart of the novels. Characters such as Fagin, Mr Micawber, Little Nell, Oliver Twist, Magwitch, Esther Summerson and many, many others seem to have an exuberance and a vitality which burn them into the memory. The controversy over Dickens' characterisation is not new. Walter Bagehot in 1858 described what he called a process of **vivification**. This represents Dickens' tendency to take one central characteristic and inflate it to the point where it seems to subsume the whole character. Two examples from *Hard Times* will suffice. There is firstly Mrs Sparsit's Roman nose to

> **KEYWORD**
>
> Vivification To take one central characteristic and inflate it to the point where it takes over the whole character.

which Dickens alludes on her every appearance in the novel and then there is Stephen Blackpool's tag-line, 'tis all a muddle' which he utters in almost every conversation. Many critics of the nineteenth and twentieth centuries were of the opinion that this type of characterisation lacked psychological depth. It seemed to belong to a tradition that was founded in the world of pantomime and melodrama rather than that of literature. This assessment has changed and is still evolving, particularly in relation to the later works, and we will return to this later in the book. Whatever the eventual conclusion of this debate (assuming that it will ever conclude), one clear reason to read a Dickens' novel is to enjoy the visual richness of his characters.

Complex plots

Another area of popular appeal is that of Dickens' plots. The twists and unfathomable (often incredible) role of coincidence have always been an attraction at the popular level; after all such resolutions are the staple diet of popular forms such as the melodrama and the 'whodunit'. Oliver, discovering that Rose Maylie, the adopted niece of the woman whose house he burgles, is really his aunt, is a wonderful example of Dickens stretching coincidence possibly beyond the realms of credibility. *Bleak House* is another example of Dickens' ability to produce intricate and interwoven plots. His deftness in doing this is made even more astounding when one remembers that the novel was written and first published in serial form under great pressure.

HUMOUR

A frequently overlooked aspect of Dickens and one which wholly commends him to the modern reader is his humour. *Hard Times* has some bleak and very dark moments yet there are also much lighter and very funny passages. The uncovering, by the unwitting Mrs Sparsit, of Bounderby's mythological childhood as being a tissue of lies, coming as it does amidst much bluster and embarrassment, is wonderfully entertaining. The modern reader of *Great Expectations* still finds the transparency of Pip's narration amusing because it allows us to see him as he cannot see himself. His foibles are human and, as such, do not change over time. The reader can feel a little smug and superior while wishing that Pip would come to his senses. We can smile at Pip's mistakes because they are of the same nature as the sort of mistakes that we make ourselves. Dickens is often much less subtle than this, showing up a character trait or an attitude by first amplifying it and then wreaking revenge. In the case of Mr Bumble in *Oliver Twist*, we are invited to enjoy his ultimate humiliation first at the hands of his wife and then by a twist of ironic fate. And of course we do.

DICKENS REVIVED

In the early part of the twentieth century Dickens' reputation waned among academics, although he still remained popular with his readers. Then in the middle of the centurycame various separate reappraisals of his work by George Orwell, Edmund Wilson and F.R. Leavis which began a process of rehabilitation. Wilson was particularly influential here, pointing to Dickens as the literary master of Dostoyevsky. He also highlighted a much more macabre aspect of the novels, particularly the later masterpieces. The publication in 1947 by the influential academic F.R. Leavis of *The Great Tradition* placing *Hard Times* firmly within the canon of English literature, also helped to re-establish Dickens as an author worthy of study. In more modern times, Dickens has been separately reappraised by cultural movements as diverse as **Structuralism** and **New Historicism**. As might be expected, **feminist**

KEYWORDS

Structuralism Intellectual movement originating in France in the 1950s in the work of Levi Straus and Roland Barthes. Stresses that things cannot be understood in isolation but need to be seen in a wider context.

New Historicism A theory which takes the view that there can be no historical certainty. The past can only be seen from within our own ideological present.

Feminism The study of gender politics from a female perspective.

writers also have plenty to say about Dickens' world view. There is something in Dickens for everybody to tease out and enjoy.

* * * *SUMMARY* * * *

- Dickens has remained a popular writer with the general reader.

- Dickens' characters burn themselves into our imagination.

- The plots of Dickens' novels are complex, often using coincidence as a means of achieving resolution.

- His humour still affects us.

- Since his rediscovery by academics in the mid twentieth century his work has been subject to continuing re-evaluation.

- There is something in Dickens for everyone.

Biography

DICKENS: THE MAN

Dickens was born on 7 February 1812 in Portsmouth to a family best described as middle-class but frequently impoverished. The social position and the wealth (or lack of it) of his family are important in helping us see what it was that drove Dickens to become the most celebrated writer of his day. The spectre of poverty and its humiliations lay behind the frequent long hours and arduous schedule which Dickens followed right up to his death on 9 June 1870.

The blacking factory

In February 1824 John Dickens, continually living beyond his means, found himself imprisoned in the Marshalsea Prison for debt. Charles, then aged 12, was sent to work at Warren's Blacking Factory. This incident was to have a profound effect on the young and sensitive boy. His life until then had been that of a young gentleman. For the young Charles, suddenly finding himself working with urchins and rough working-class lads was a huge psychological trauma. He wrote in his unfinished autobiography: 'No words can express the secret agony of my soul as I sunk into this companionship.'

This time at the blacking factory provides insight into the feverish drive that motivated Dickens. It provides an explanation for the huge number of abandoned children and orphans in his work, characters such as Oliver Twist, Pip and David Copperfield. It also lies behind grossly sentimental fairy-tale endings where the poor, suffering boy is finally rescued from poverty and servitude often by a kindly, rich gentleman.

There are three further notes of significance to add about this time in Dickens' life. The first is the huge betrayal Dickens felt when his mother wanted to send him back to the blacking factory even after his father's release from prison. The second is that Dickens himself attached great importance to his childhood and believed strongly that his personal past exerted an influence on both his writing and his personality. The third is that the tale of his childhood was a source of both shame and fascination to him. Too ashamed to tell his children about the blacking factory, he nevertheless used the memories in one way or another in almost every novel he wrote.

Parliamentary reporter

When the family finally managed to climb out of debt, Dickens became a day pupil at a school in London from 1824 to 1827. At 15, he began work as an office boy at an attorney's. Here, like David Copperfield, he studied shorthand at night and eventually was able to become a freelance reporter at Doctor's Commons Courts, a position which was to make him very cynical about the workings both of parliament and the law.

First love

In 1830 he met and fell in love with his first love, Maria Beadnell. Like many first loves it was an intense infatuation that, sadly for the 19-year-old Dickens, was not reciprocated. From many accounts, Maria was a pretty, much admired young lady with many suitors, most of whom seemed to have more prospects than the young Dickens. In this relationship it is likely we have the origins of both Estella of *Great Expectations* and Dora of *David Copperfield.*

Second love and marriage

In 1834, he adopted the soon-to-be famous pseudonym Boz. In the following year he met and became engaged to Catherine Hogarth. They married in April 1836, a marriage that was to last for 22 years. Accounts of the happiness and success of the marriage vary. Most agree that for the first ten to twelve years the couple were fairly happy. Catherine suffered badly from post-natal depression which, given that she produced eight children, cannot have made life very easy. There is a sense too that they slowly grew apart. Catherine was by nature a cautious, nervous person, sometimes slow to act. Dickens was, by contrast, almost maniacally fast in his thinking, with a restless, often intemperate nature.

During the marriage he changed a great deal. He grew from being an unknown struggling writer to the famous, the adored, the acclaimed, Mr Charles Dickens. The relationship became extremely unbalanced. Their marriage was also odd in that it was one shared for much of the time on a strictly platonic basis by either Mary or Georgina, Catherine's two sisters.

The sisters-in-law

Mary was Catherine's younger sister and had been her chaperone during her engagement. After the marriage, Mary lived with Charles and Catherine but in May 1937, after returning with them from the theatre, she was suddenly taken ill and died in Dickens' arms. This was to prove highly formative. Her death was devastating for the young Dickens, and while much writing has exaggerated her importance, it is true nonetheless that she was idealised by the young and imaginative writer. It is thought, for example, that Mary is the origin of the many virginal and highly romanticised young women who occur so frequently in Dickens' works.

Georgina was described by Dickens in his will as 'the best and truest friend man ever had'. Her role, by today's standards, is an extraordinary one. She lived with the Dickens family from the age of 15. She acted as Catherine's companion, the children's nursemaid, and as a companion for Dickens himself. When the marriage finally failed she remained loyal to Dickens, continuing to live with him at Gad's Hill, where she defied public opinion and carried on running the household. After his death she seems to have performed the role of his grieving widow, keeping alive the memory of the great man. While speculation has always run amok, there is no evidence of any sexual or romantic engagement with Dickens during the whole of this time. It may well be that the sisterly women (Esther Summerson in *Bleak House*, for example), who seem so attractive in the novels, are modelled on Georgina.

DICKENS' NATURE

Dickens appears to have been a very complex man, full of those contradictions that seem to mark men of genius. His was undoubtedly a very sensitive nature yet it was also one that could be totally obtuse. Most certainly he lacked what we might call today 'personal insight'. He found it impossible to admit that he may be in the wrong. It was always the fault of another. This was most notable in the break-up of his marriage, where he laid the blame wholly upon Catherine, seemingly blind to the fact that by this time, at the age of 46, he was involved, almost certainly romantically, with an attractive 18-year-old actress named Ellen Ternan.

His was also a very driven nature. He worked phenomenally hard, producing novels, short stories and articles to order, often meeting impossible deadlines. Through all this he continued to edit substantial magazines, carry out charity work and, particularly in the later years, to undertake arduous lectures and readings.

CULT OF PERSONALITY

One aspect of Dickens that has been touched upon by many biographers, is the cult of personality that Dickens quite consciously developed. Forster, his earliest biographer, writes:

> Undoubtedly one of the impressions [he leaves] is that of the intensity and tenacity with which he recognised, realised, contemplated, cultivated and thoroughly enjoyed his own individuality in even its most trivial manifestations.

> Forster, J., *The Life of Charles Dickens*, Dent (1928), p.818

When we read about Dickens, even his personal letters, it becomes clear that he was consciously self-dramatising, making himself into what he wanted the world to see. This is echoed in *Great Expectations* where Pip self-consciously constructs himself in his own misguided image.

ELLEN TERNAN

At the age of 46 Dickens, who had had many friendships with different women over the years, met and fell in love with an 18-year-old actress, Ellen Ternan. She was pretty, intelligent and self-willed and Dickens seems to have become totally and irretrievably infatuated with her. This was the final blow to his marriage; he and Catherine parted in 1858.

In 1865, while returning from France with Mrs Ternan and Ellen, Dickens took the 2.38pm tidal train from Folkstone to London. Just before Staplehurst the train was derailed as it passed over a viaduct because of works on the line. It was a terrible accident in which many were killed. Six of the first-class carriages plummeted down into the riverbed. Only the carriage in which Dickens travelled remained coupled to the second-class part of the train and the travellers, much shaken, were able to climb out. By all accounts, Dickens, behaviour at the accident was most courageous: he attended to the dying and the injured with great calm and presence of mind. The incident, however, left him emotionally very scarred and, despite his many efforts, also added to the public knowledge of his affair with Ellen.

The affair lasted until Dickens' death, forcing him to lead a difficult double life, with Ellen eventually living in a house in Peckham, his estranged wife and elder son living in Camden Town and Dickens and the rest of the family living at Gad's Hill.

WORSENING HEALTH

During the middle to late 1860s Dickens' health began to worsen. Even so he continued to work at a punishing pace. During 1869, he continued giving readings in England, Scotland and Ireland, until at last he collapsed, showing symptoms of a mild stroke. While giving further provincial readings, he still insisted on working and began writing *The Mystery of Edwin Drood*.

Dickens' final public readings took place in London in 1870. He suffered another stroke on 8 June at Gad's Hill, after a full day's work on *Edwin Drood*, and died the next day. He was buried at Westminster Abbey on 14 June, and the last episode of the unfinished *Edwin Drood* appeared in September.

Dickens was famous for his dramatic readings.

POPULARITY OF DICKENS

It is hard for us to imagine a novelist enjoying the degree of fame and popularity that Dickens achieved. His face was most certainly instantly recognisable, he was more or less worshipped by the provincial lower middle classes, and he was undoubtedly a 'great man' at a time when the worship of great men was widespread. His death was an occasion for national mourning. His grave at Poets Corner in Westminster Abbey was laid open for two days during which time there was a continuous stream of mourners paying their respects. His death marked the passing of a period – of great change and social upheaval but also a period which he himself helped to shape. Just as we today see much of Victorian England through the characters and landscapes created by Dickens, so too did the Victorians see themselves as shaped and reflected by the pen of their greatest novelist.

✳ ✳ ✳ ✳*SUMMARY* ✳ ✳ ✳ ✳

- Dickens' early childhood experiences of family debt and working in the blacking factory were formative.

- He cut his teeth as a parliamentary reporter – another formative experience.

- His first love was Maria Beadnell who did not return his affection and who became the basis for Estella and Dora.

- He married his second love, Catherine Hogarth, the marriage lasting 22 years.

- They shared the marital home with Catherine's two sisters, one of whom died in Dickens' arms.

- He had a long affair when Ellen Ternan, 22 years his junior.

- Dickens was careful to construct a self-dramatising persona.

The Victorian Scene

DICKENS AS A VICTORIAN NOVELIST

We tend to think of Dickens as both a London writer and as a Victorian. Neither of these assumptions is quite correct. He was born some 25 years before Victoria's accession to the throne and died over 30 years before her. The vast majority of his writing and all of his novels were, however, published during her reign.

Victoria		Accession 1837		Died 1901
Dickens	Born 1812		Died 1870	

While so much of his work is set in London he was neither born there nor did he live in the capital for much of his life. For that matter not much of his writing was completed there. Yet it is his dramatic portrayals of London life, particularly its crime, disease and poverty, for which he is best remembered.

URBANISATION AND ITS EFFECTS

During Dickens' lifetime there had been a huge population shift from the countryside to the town. In the 1801 census only 30 percent of the population lived in towns; by the 1851 census this had risen to nearly 50 percent. London itself had grown from just over one million inhabitants to two and a half million in the same period. Dickens was acutely aware of the social effects of this expansion.

Certainly the impoverished conditions of the poor and particularly the terrible sufferings of children were issues that remained close to his heart throughout his life. His first public readings were prompted by a desire to improve hospital facilities for children in the capital. It is a theme that he returns to repeatedly in the novels. The terrible sufferings of Oliver Twist both in the workhouse and on the streets of London, the abject poverty of Jo the crossing sweeper in *Bleak House* and the poor housing of the working man in *Hard Times* are just three examples of this concern.

Another effect of urbanisation was that the crowded and dirty conditions of the poor allowed disease to spread with alarming rapidity. The Thames, for example, has been described as little better than an open sewer, was polluted by London's untreated sewage. There were huge differences in the ways in which people lived. There was a deep divide between the West End of London where the middle classes lived and the East End where the poor lived. It was a society deeply divided by wealth, class and gender.

Dickens was concerned by the criminality which was concomitant with poverty and neglect. The world of Fagin was a reality, as Dickens was at pains to point out. Crime and prostitution were never far away in the urban scene.

FAMILY

In understanding the presentation of family in Victorian society we have to distinguish between the family as portrayed by the prevailing dominant ideology and the reality. The fiction of the family was that it was strong, harmonious, safe and firmly hierarchical, with the man as the head and his wife as confidante, support, mother to his children and housekeeper. The reality, of course, was often very different. For a start, families then were as diverse as families are today. Certainly middle-class families were under pressure to conform but, as Dickens' own marriage shows, they frequently failed to live up to this ideal. Dickens depicted many dysfunctional families as we shall see later on.

MEN AND WOMEN

At the heart of the family lay a strong belief in separate roles for men and women. It led to entirely different sets of moral codes being applied to men and women, an aspect of Victorian society that today we would regard as unbearably hypocritical. The dominant ideology of the period saw men and women as fundamentally different both physiologically and emotionally. Ideas which separate gender (masculine and feminine) from biological sex (male and female) would have been unknown to the majority of people in Victorian society. Men and women were different and did different things. To men went the guardianship of work and industry as well as such other interests as politics and law. To women belonged guardianship of the home and hearth. In their responsibility for running the household and care of the children they were often assisted by nannies, servants and other domestic help, dependent upon the income and social class of the family. In poorer families women would also have to go to work and were usually treated very badly and exploited.

Women who did try to move out of the domestic sphere into male preserves were frequently satirised by Dickens (for example Mrs Pardiggle and Mrs Jellyby in *Bleak House*). A study of Victorian female dress shows how impractical it was for performing many 'men's' jobs and how it emphasised the Victorian notion of 'femininity' which encompassed vulnerability, virtue (repressed sexuality), faithfulness and subservience. The Victorian woman vowed to 'love, honour and obey' her husband.

This inequality of the sexes was taken as a matter of course in the 1830s and although it gradually changed over the century, the perceived view is that Dickens remained rooted in his 'sexist' prejudices. A kinder interpretation is that Dickens was merely reflecting the social paradigm of his age.

To us today Victorian England seems sexually repressed. Even piano legs were covered in polite society although illicit sex carried on as usual. This points to a hypocrisy in the realm of sexual mores. It also led to double standards. Transgression of the strict sexual codes could enhance a man's masculinity while any deviant sexual behaviour among women was equated with a lack of femininity and with sinfulness. The dire consequences for women who transgressed this code of behaviour are explored in many of Dickens' novels. Look, for example, at Little Emily in *David Copperfield* or Lady Dedlock in *Bleak House*.

CLASS STRUCTURE

Class was a sensitive and ongoing issue for Dickens. The huge movements of population into the towns and the rise of a new middle class had a tremendous impact on the very rigid class structure that had existed in England since medieval times. This theme is explored by many Victorian novelists. It is seen at its most vivid when Dickens is exploring the process of characters moving between class boundaries. There is the crass Mr Bounderby in *Hard Times* with his rags to riches tale used by Dickens to satirise the issue, and there is Esther's often very ambiguous social position in *Bleak House*. Perhaps the most observant account of the transition from lower to middle class is the tale of Pip in *Great Expectations*. The scenes of Pip learning how to eat, drink and fold a napkin from his new friend Herbert are both highly amusing and an interesting insight into what it meant to be a gentleman.

THE TRANSPORT REVOLUTION

Another feature of Victorian England was the incredible expansion in mobility occasioned by the spread of the railways. The rate of development of the railways is astonishing: the first railway from London to Manchester was begun in 1830 and by 1850 there were over 6000 miles of track connecting towns across England. Movement from town to town or country to town had previously been very difficult, indeed in the winter it was often impossible. Journeys by coach and horses were long and uncomfortable. The railways transformed this and did so in a remarkably short time. Compare, for example, the difficulty and tedium of travel described in *Bleak House* set at the start of the century and *Hard Times* set in the 1850s, where the railway permits Bounderby's mother the opportunity to visit Coketown once each year to witness the opulence of her son (and eventually to unmask him).

DICKENS AND HIS AUDIENCE

All Dickens' novels were produced first in serial form and published in a range of family magazines including *Bentley's Miscellany* and *Household Words*. They were usually published in monthly parts although some such as *Hard Times* were published weekly. An interesting aspect of this process was that as Dickens published the instalments he received feedback from his readers. This sometimes led to changes in plot and characterisation. The monthly sales figures of *Household Words* averaged around 40,000 copies although it did at times rise to 100,000. The majority of the readers of this magazine and the 40 or so other similar publications in circulation were largely from the relatively new middle classes, although it would also have been read by many of the skilled working class. In contrast, it should be remembered that in 1850 around a quarter of the population (about eight million people) would have been illiterate.

DICKENS THE SOCIAL REFORMER

The Victorian age was one of marked contrasts in wealth, class, sexuality, gender and health. There was much social injustice and Dickens, above all else, saw himself as a reformer – a champion of justice in an unjust world.

＊＊＊＊SUMMARY＊＊＊＊

- The population of the cities rose inexorably during the period. Levels of poverty and disease also rose dramatically. Crime was a way of life for many.

- The idealisation of the family and the importance of family values was central to the way the Victorian middle classes saw themselves. The reality may well have been somewhat different.

- Men and women were seen as having separate roles in a patriarchal structure.

- The expression of sexuality was different for men and women.

- The rigidity and conventions of the class system are frequently explored within the novels of Dickens and other Victorian novelists.

- The impact of the railways upon geographical mobility was immense.

- Dickens was a hugely popular novelist and highly influential figure within his own period.

- Dickens' novels were all published in serial form and were sometimes affected by the feedback from his readers.

How to Read Dickens

READ FOR PLEASURE

Dickens is fun. Read him for pleasure. Dickens' novels are great entertainment. He set out to write interesting stories and he peopled them with fascinating characters and a wealth of incident. The more you read of him the more you will get to like his style and his characters. A certain fondness grows for characters one remembers from previous reading, or from films. Re-reading a Dickens novel is like meeting old friends.

There is pleasure to be found in so many aspects of his writings: in his characters; in the detailed descriptions of London; in his themes, particularly in his fight against injustice; in his comic writing; in his wondrously complex and often surprising plots; and in the landscapes he creates for his characters to inhabit.

One surprising realisation for the reader new to Dickens lies in his exceptionally wide range of written styles. He is capable of sustained atmospheric writing, full of suspense and sense of place as in the short story *The Signalman*; high relief caricature as in *Hard Times*; sustained 'romantic' narrative as in *Great Expectations*; and rich complex satire such as in *Bleak House*.

Dickens obtained great enjoyment from the names of his characters: Mr Bumble, Jaggers, Smallweed, M'Choakumchild, Wackford Squeers, Estella, Pumblechook, Murdstone, Gradgrind, Bounderby; the list is endless. Many names provide metaphorical insights into the character of the person named, and all are part of a glorious invention. They are to be savoured and treasured.

READ BEYOND REALITY

Don't expect Dickens to be fully representational. Behind most of his work lies his desire to expose the hypocrite, the cruel, the unfeeling, the vain, the self-deceived, the unthinking and the self-centred. In order to do this Dickens goes beyond pure realism, often exaggerating character or plot to make his points.

In *Oliver Twist*, Dickens creates a powerful picture of the effects of the 1834 Poor Laws. There is an obvious exaggeration in every scene in the workhouse. He exaggerates the prominence of the Beadle, to show the potential for corruption; and he heightens the pomposity of Mr Bumble and the shrewishness of his wife. In general he makes the system of parish relief look appalling. In doing so, by employing an ironic overstatement, he achieves his objective by exciting his readers' sense of outrage; and he does so in a way that a 'realistic' rendering may not have achieved.

Dickens murders Nancy (again).

READ THE EXPERTS

Many modern editions of the works include excellent introductions by experts. They can be read with interest before or after reading a particular novel (or both). Each contains a different insight and useful background material.

This *Beginner's Guide* contains references to works of commentary and criticism. Some are of the esoteric academic type and will need to be read with patience and fortitude several times, while others provide excellent background, invaluable information and perceptive insight in a more accessible way. A recent survey in a large university library revealed over 300 different texts of commentary, biography and criticism about Dickens, some out of date, many thumbed almost to extinction but all with useful things to say.

READ THE BOOKS

Although books like this one can help you to find a way into authors and their works, they can only act as guides and are not a substitute for the real thing. As part of your studies, read Dickens as much as you can, whenever you can. And enjoy.

* * * *SUMMARY* * * *

- Read for pleasure. At one level at least the novels can be seen as 'entertainments' full of suspense, humour and astonishingly vivid characterisation.

- Read the experts – there are a fair number of them out there.

- Above all, read the books.

- Read beyond reality and try not to expect a wholly realistic portrait of Victorian life.

5 Some Major Themes

Dickens has created for us a world that has infused itself into the popular imagination. The very word 'Dickensian' has become synonymous with a popular view of the Victorian world. It conjures up both a dark world full of social injustice, poor education, criminality and exploitation and also a lighter, more sentimental world in which the family gathers contentedly around the hearth and where kindly gentlemen rescue poor orphans from certain destitution. Here Christmas is represented by a fat sizzling goose and the glowing benevolence of the reformed Ebenezer Scrooge. Like elsewhere in the Dickens legend, we can be certain that whatever stereotypical themes we have inherited from his fiction they are certain to be both contradictory and complex.

Recent academic thinking has moved us away from seeing Dickens as a polarised critic of social injustice, taking strong stands and using one viewpoint about all matters of concern. Most modern writing about literature explores the complexities and tensions within the texts, and examines ambiguities and paradoxes. Once the reader does this, it becomes clear that Dickens cannot be said to represent a set of unchanging and fixed values, indeed his texts often contain contradictory ideas and views. Dickens is as much a product of his time as anyone else, and consequently is as likely to be as inconsistent, prejudiced and short-sighted as his contemporaries. For example, his rather limited view of the family and what it could achieve was forged in the moral, religious, social, political and ethical ethos of his time.

THE GREATEST EVIL

Poverty was for Dickens the great evil. The neglect of the poor was the worst of the many crimes he accused those in power of committing. For Dickens, it was the duty of the wealthy to take responsibility for the prevention and ultimate cure of such social ills. It was a duty that he, as the most famous writer of his generation, took very seriously. He felt that his wealth and fame brought with it a duty to make the public aware of social evils such as poverty; homelessness; failures in law or the delays inherent in the Court of Chancery; failures in educational provision and methodology; and, most important of all to Dickens, failures in the way society looked after the children of the poor.

There are many examples of destitute and ill-treated children in the novels. Jo, the parentless and homeless crossing sweeper in *Bleak House*, is the first fully articulated representative of the street child. Here we are shown the awful and logical conclusion of ignorance and poverty on the mind of a child:

> Name, Jo. Nothing else that he knows on. Don't know that everybody has two names. Never heerd of sich a think. Don't know that Jo is short for a longer name. Thinks it long enough for HIM. HE don't find no fault with it. Spell it? No. HE can't spell it. No father, no mother, no friends. Never been to school. What's home? Knows a broom's a broom, and knows it's wicked to tell a lie. Don't recollect who told him about the broom or about the lie, but knows both. Can't exactly say what'll be done to him arter he's dead if he tells a lie to the gentlemen here, but believes it'll be something wery bad to punish him, and serve him right – and so he'll tell the truth.

> *Bleak House*, Chapter 11

The inevitable outcome of such a childhood is shown most vividly in the fate of Jo and is reinforced in later novels. Take, for example, Magwitch's account of his childhood in *Great Expectations*:

> I've been locked up, as much as a silver tea-kettle. I've been carted here and carted there, and put out of this town and put out of that town, and stuck in the stocks, and whipped and worried and drove. I've no more notion where I was born, than you have – if so much. I first become aware of myself, down in Essex, a thieving turnips for my living. Summun had run away from me – a man – a tinker – and he'd took the fire with him, and left me wery cold.

> *Great Expectations*, Chapter 42

For Dickens these were not failures in parenting but rather the wider failure of a society that allowed such deprivation. For him poverty and neglect and ignorance led inevitably to crime and prostitution. Improved social conditions, better housing and sanitation were essential prerequisites for a civilised country. Once these were in place then education was the key, or rather the catalyst, for change.

EDUCATION: FACT OR FANCY

Education and how to handle it had been a subject for debate (and confusion) for nearly the whole of the first half of the nineteenth century and continued to be so during Dickens' time. Dickens was very much engaged with this debate.

Malcolm Andrews summarises the dilemma of the period:

> The problem may, for convenience, be briefly summarised as follows. Should the naturally imaginative mind of the child be allowed to develop freely, nourished by romance and fairy tale, or should it be disciplined early to enable it to meet the demands of the real world in which it will have to function as a rational, mature adult?
>
> *Dickens and the Grown-Up Child*, Macmillan (1994), p. 5

This is a theme which is explored in considerable detail in *Hard Times*, the shortest of Dickens' novels. By this time in his life Dickens would seem to have come down heavily in favour of what he termed '**Fancy**', a term

KEYWORD

Fancy Dickens' term for creative imagination.

which, as Slater (1999) points out, was for Dickens always synonymous with creative imagination. It was a positive force in life and, as in the case of Sleary's Circus in *Hard Times*, a healing and redeeming force. Fancy represents all that is rendered worthless in Utilitarian philosophy.

Hard Times and its biting satirical portrayal of a utilitarian education was Dickens' highly critical response to the government-funded training colleges for teachers which laid great emphasis upon the acquisition of factual knowledge. The point is rammed home in the opening paragraph of the novel:

> NOW, what I want is, Facts. Teach these boys and girls nothing but Facts. Facts alone are wanted in life. Plant nothing else, and root out everything else. You can only form the minds of reasoning animals upon Facts: nothing else will ever be of any service to them. This is the principle on which I bring up my own children, and this is the principle on which I bring up these children. Stick to Facts, sir!
>
> *Hard Times*, Part 1, Chapter 1

Yet a factually based education is shown to be brutal, short-sighted, and morally unsound. It leads Louisa into an unhappy marriage and Tom into thievery. Bitzer, the very model of Gradgrindian success, is shown to be nothing more than an unfeeling, self-centred bigot who betrays Gradgrind by the means of his own philosophy.

> 'Bitzer,' said Mr. Gradgrind, broken down, and miserably submissive to him, 'have you a heart?'
>
> 'The circulation, sir,' returned Bitzer, smiling at the oddity of the question, 'couldn't be carried on without one. No man, sir, acquainted with the facts established by Harvey relating to the circulation of the blood, can doubt that I have a heart.'
>
> *Hard Times*, Part 3, Chapter 8

For Dickens, writing in an age before universal education and rigorous inspection, schooling seems to have been rather a desultory affair at best, often leading to cruelty and neglect. Schools such as Dotheboys Hall in *Nicholas Nickleby* or Salem House in *Great Expectations* proffer a meagre educational content and seem to be designed only for the purpose of inflicting pain on their pupils. Institutional education in the Dickensian world appears to be more for the benefit of the masters of the school, and is something done *to* children, a form of social training by punishment, rather than having any enlightening purpose.

THE FAMILY

The family was at the centre of the Victorian social ideal. Despite his own feelings of betrayal concerning his parents, Dickens saw the family unit as a method of salvation.

As if to make this point, the vast majority of families presented by Dickens in the novels are highly dysfunctional. Mrs Gargery's raising of Pip 'by hand' in *Great Expectations*, the Gradgrinds in *Hard Times*, the Hexams in *Our Mutual Friend*, the Jellybys in *Bleak House*; every novel seems to have, often at the heart of it, a highly dysfunctional family. Yet two points are important to note here. First, these 'bad' families are almost universally condemned within the narrative. Dickens presents them as moral lessons in how children should *not* be raised. Second, as Tolstoy notes, happy families do not make for good fiction.

LOST LITTLE BOYS AND OTHER ORPHANS

Dickens wrote several works which might be said to be novels of identity and of the effects of life experience on the development of the child. Many of his stories concern the waif-child, the innocent without history cast into the world to take his or her fate as it comes.

Dickens championed orphans, waifs and strays.

In *Great Expectations*, we have Pip, an orphan, growing out of his situation through a combination of unforeseen circumstances (Magwitch's plans, Miss Havisham's interventions), social aspiration, self-deception and, ultimately, self-realisation. In *Hard Times*, another orphan child, Sissy Jupe, is rescued and becomes a quiet force for good in the novel. Likewise David Copperfield is orphaned early and, after suffering at the hands of Mrs and Miss Murdstone, eventually makes good under the stewardship of Betsy Trotwood. Oliver Twist is the classic Dickens orphan, forced into criminality before being redeemed.

Malcolm Andrews (op cit), isolates several types of grown-up child. There is the Professional Infant, such as Miss Ninetta Crummles in *Nicholas Nickleby*; the child with Arrested Development such as Barnaby Rudge; or Premature Little Adults, such as the Artful Dodger in *Oliver Twist* or the Smallweed children in *Bleak House*; Little Mothers and Housekeepers, such as Little Dorrit (or perhaps Sissy Jupe); and the Child-Like Gentleman, such as Joe Gargery, and Dr Strong in *David Copperfield*.

The issue of childhood and its development is thus central to Dickens' work. *David Copperfield*, the 'favourite child' among Dickens' fictional offspring, is the novel that most strikingly demonstrates the issue of how far childhood may be regarded as a virtue or a defeat. Andrews points out that *David Copperfield* is the first of the novels to chart the psychological journey from child-state to adult-state in any detail. We can clearly see that in a lot of the earlier works, children had not been allowed to develop: characters such as Smike, Oliver, Little Nell and Tiny Tim exist to serve an artistic purpose – that of embodying Dickens' intention stated in the preface of *Oliver Twist*, to show the principle of 'good' triumphing over adverse circumstance. After *David Copperfield*, characters are often allowed to grow and develop, often in the School of Life, Pip in *Great Expectations* being a notable example.

SOCIAL CLASS

Dickens was much preoccupied with questions of social class. Here, as elsewhere, there would seem to be a confusion of standards. As Kate Flint notes in discussing Dickens' attitude towards class, his intensely angry attacks on social conditions were 'coupled with an apparent resistance to the idea of any alteration to the class structure' (*Dickens*, Harvester (1986), p. 18). Indeed his novels often depict a world where the middle classes offer a possible haven of gentility and kindness, free from base desires and criminality. This is at its most obvious in *Oliver Twist* where we are continually reminded that it is Oliver's true pedigree which prevents him from succumbing to the corrupting devices of Fagin and his mob. Oliver's impeccable speech, which is different from that of Claypole, Bumble or Fagin, and his innocent angelic features are paraded before us throughout the whole novel. Catherine Waters comments:

> It is highly significant for the politics of the family in this novel that his innate goodness and his genealogy are indisputably written in his face, for the appeal to nature involved in their reading draws on a conception of the family that is based on aristocratic premises to legitimate middle-class origins.

> Waters, C., *Dickens and the Politics of the Family*, CUP, (1997) p. 31

She goes on to argue that Oliver is so obviously shown as originating from a pedigree so different from that of the criminal classes who conspire to corrupt him, that social class is highlighted as a major theme within the novel. It is a novel where the social divide is also a moral divide. The middle-class gentility of the Brownlows and Maylies is shown as a deliberate contrast to the seedy immorality of Sikes and Fagin. Monks is more of a problem. His middle-class background places him awkwardly in the world of the villains. Perhaps this is why he, among all the rogues in the novel, is allowed to escape his just deserts.

In *Bleak House* we see many of the strata of Victorian society. We can observe clearly the constraints imposed by a hierarchical class system.

The upper classes are represented first by Lord and Lady Dedlock, shown very consciously here as both decayed and corrupt. This class is also represented by the humorously named Lords Boodle, Doodle, Foodle, etc. It raises again Dickens' obsession with responsibility; wealth and title brings with it great power and it is the responsibility of those so endowed to use their power with humanity and compassion.

The middle classes are represented by the world of John Jarndyce. He is the model of wealthy philanthropy which Dickens so admired. Yet even he is shown to be misguided at times with, for instance, his support for Skimpole, the scrounging, self-centred child-man. Dickens also shows very clearly the barriers which he perceived as existing between the social classes. It is shown most vividly in the visit by Mrs Pardiggle and her entourage to the brickmaker's cottage. Esther and Ada feel 'intrusive and out of place' and while Mrs Pardiggle seems to remain oblivious to the sensibilities of those around her, Esther comments:

> We both felt painfully sensible that between us and these people there
> was an iron barrier which could not be removed by our new friend.
>
> *Bleak House*, Chapter 8

Whatever the intentions of Mrs Pardiggle, and Dickens is scathing in his appraisal of these, the effect of her intrusion into the home of a poor family is to cross the line that marks out the very strong divisions between social classes. It is only Inspector Bucket, *Bleak House*'s enigmatic detective, who is able to cross these barriers as he 'pervades a vast number of houses and strolls about an infinity of streets'. Only he, it would seem, is able to step across the invisible but ever present barrier of class.

INJUSTICE
The constant thread through all the novels which links all the other themes together is injustice. This injustice is displayed most strongly by institutions such as parliament, local government, industry or the law. In this sense, all of Dickens' work can be said to be subsumed under it.

＊ ＊ ＊ ＊*SUMMARY* ＊ ＊ ＊ ＊

- Some of Dickens' major themes are:

  - Poverty and neglect. Poverty is identified as the greatest evil; it is seen by Dickens as a failure of society in general and of those in power in particular.

  - Education. Dickens abhorred Utilitarian education which he believed stifled imagination and creativity.

  - The salvation of the innocent.

  - Social class. Many of the novels explore this theme although Dickens position often seems to be deeply contradictory.

  - Injustice is the theme which links the other themes together.

Major Works 1: Four novels 6

GENERAL

In this chapter we will look at four of the novels spanning the early to middle years of Dickens' writing career: *Oliver Twist*, *David Copperfield*, *Hard Times* and *Great Expectations*. In this way we can see how some of his themes were worked through in practice. A full list of his works and their dates of publication can be found in the Chronology of major works at the end of this book. It is instructive but not essential to follow the development of his style and preoccupations by reading the novels in order of writing. A discussion of *Bleak House* can be found in the next chapter.

A general characteristic of the novels is their complex and often convoluted plots. They largely follow a linear and chronological order of events but several strands are spun together and unsuspected relationships between the characters are revealed. Even *Great Expectations*, which to many seems fairly straightforward – the story of Pip and his growth into mature adulthood – contains the stories of Magwitch, Compeyson, Joe Gargery, Miss Havisham and Estella.

Dickens has been criticised because of the arbitrary way in which characters suddenly find they are related in some way. Thankfully, modern criticism has moved away from attacking Dickens for stylistic reasons: his love of 'coincidence'; the tortuous turns of his narratives; and his over-exaggerated characters; and has become generally much less plot fixated. Experience tells us that life is a muddle, a series of chance moments and encounters, of unexpected happenings good and bad. We say that 'it's a small world' to explain this phenomenon, and, when down on our luck, are often of the same mind as the Micawbers, trusting that something will turn up. Sometimes it does. And so it does in Dickens, to the surprise of Oliver and Pip to name but two.

Dickens' novels express his strong social conscience but do not overtly give answers. For example, he has no panacea for the ills of the workhouse and Poor Law system: Oliver finds peace through the intercessions of the kindly world of Mr Brownlow and a newfound family, plus £3000 to set him up. The dreadful Mr and Mrs Bumble are made to suffer the fate of becoming inmates in their own workhouse. Bill Sikes suffers horrific visions and accidentally but aptly hangs himself. Thus although some kind of justice and retribution are meted out, no other solutions to society's ills are offered.

Ironically, Dickens' anger at poor social conditions and his contempt for legal and political processes were accompanied by a complete resistance to any suggestion that the rigid class structure of the Victorian period should be altered. Class and money become the sources of salvation for his characters, as, indeed, they were for Dickens himself. Modern critical theory has moved away from seeing this as a fault in Dickens.

OLIVER TWIST

Oliver Twist was begun in 1837 as a serialisation in *Bentley's Miscellany*. It marks the beginning of Dickens' career as a pure novelist although, of course, he had been a writer (journalism, sketches, short stories and the *Pickwick Papers*) since 1833. It was the first novel in the English language to take a child character as a hero.

It was not initially introduced as a novel, either because Dickens fought shy of the notion, or because he wasn't entirely sure how the work might develop. In letters of the time he referred to the first instalments as a 'paper'.

Social conscience

The novel announced Dickens as the voice of the social conscience of the period, particularly the scenes in the workhouse which were rightly interpreted as a scathing indictment of the new Poor Law of 1834. Of course, as the novel developed it moved away from the effects of the Poor Law and into the dark world of urban criminality, but the first few chapters were so strong and extraordinary that the scene where

Dickens introduces Oliver to Mr Bumble.

'Oliver asks for more' etched itself permanently into the collective consciousness. The workhouse came to represent the cruelties and injustices of the system and the kind of corrupt petty tyranny that the Poor Laws ushered in, most notably enshrined in the figure of Mr Bumble, the Beadle.

THE POOR LAWS

Eligibility for the receipt of help from the parish was based on two principles. First there was the 'workhouse test', which meant that you had to be able-bodied and must work for your keep, thus demonstrating true destitution (no work – no help). Second came the category of 'less eligibility', where those genuinely destitute but unable to work were put up at the parish's expense. The diet in workhouses was kept deliberately meagre as part of a policy of making life inside unattractive to the long stayer. It would have differed from parish to parish but would have consisted mostly of gruel plus the odd potato and piece of cheese. Dickens **parodies** this to make his point by suggesting that in Oliver's workhouse, the diet consisted of 'an onion twice a week, and half a roll on Sundays'. Life was harsh and starvation was a real threat.

The publication of *Oliver Twist* coincided with great deal of press coverage and criticism in *The Times* and *Morning Chronicle* over the operation of the 1834 Poor Law. In 1837, the year of first publication, a bad winter followed a poor harvest and this was exacerbated by a deepening trade depression. The first few chapters caught the public mood and helped fuel the Anti-Poor Law campaign.

KEYWORD

Parody Work in which themes and/or the style of a particular work/ author are exaggerated or applied inappropriately for the purposes of ridicule.

Good triumphing over evil

However, Dickens couldn't afford to keep the subject of his work so focused on such a narrow theme which could easily date, and so the novel developed in other ways. Dickens tells us, in his preface to the 1841 edition, that he wished to show 'in little Oliver, the principle of Good surviving through every adverse circumstance'. In this way he was able to examine the London underworld in particular detail.

Realism and reality

Of course, showing life like it is is not the same as using 'realism'. In order to entertain and make his points, Dickens exaggerates plot and character. He invents a nightmarish world full of grotesques, a world as psychologically disturbing as Grimm's fairy tales, where there is a constant threat of danger. His characters, Fagin, Artful Dodger, Sikes, and Monks in particular, are much larger than life, assuming the exaggerated proportions of the cartoon or the caricature. This is partly why the book is so disturbing, because it perturbs our subconscious mind. Characterisation steps into parody.

Take, for example, the scene where the Artful Dodger is put before the magistrate's court. Dickens cannot help using him to take a pot shot at the judicial system, which the Dodger does by taking over the proceedings, treating everyone with great disdain and declaring 'I'm an Englishman, ain't I? Where are my priwileges?' The act of this ruffian claiming his birthright puts the whole court to shame although it doesn't save him from his fate.

In a different way, Dickens can poke fun at all petty tyrants in general, and the whole parish relief system in particular, by portraying the Beadle in a series of hilarious incidents, with Mr Bumble becoming more and more pompous before being finally deflated and humiliated.

In order to appreciate fully the depth and complexity of character portrayed by Dickens, one needs to read the novel rather than rely on other interpretations. The Fagin and Bill Sikes of the book are more subtle and perhaps more frightening than the various incarnations on film and television. Dickens' Fagin is physically weak and relies on subterfuge, psychological manipulation and cunning to survive. Bill Sikes is entirely amoral and self-centred: his feelings for Nancy are devoid of emotional warmth and are an extension of his total self-centredness. To be in a room with Sikes is to be in fear of his unpredictability and brutishness. His lack of any compassion is clearly shown by his murder of Nancy and attempted murder of his other most devoted companion, his dog.

Class – a force for good or evil?
Class becomes the main force for good in the tale. Arnold Kettle in his *Introduction to the English Novel* makes the point that up until Chapter 11 Oliver is a poor boy struggling against an inhumane world. After he wakes up in Mr Brownlow's bed he has changed into young bourgeois who has been cheated of his property.

The book explores two worlds: that of Brownlow-Maylie, one of middle-class luxuriance, sound moral values, proper families; contrasted with the corrupt and ghastly world of Fagin where crime flourishes through deprivation.

Plot
The plot of the novel is usually seen as overcomplicated and unsatisfactory. It relies on a number of extraordinary coincidences: for example, the two robberies in which Oliver is forced to participate are against, first, his father's best friend and, second, his mother's sister's guardian! We must, however, get beyond a simplistic reading of this sort if we are to appreciate the book fully.

Life and death
In this, his first novel, we can savour various things. There is the struggle of little Oliver to overcome seemingly hopeless odds, and there are a wealth of interesting characters, incidents and places – Oliver's walk through London with Bill Sikes and the description of Jacob's Island being two vivid examples. The novel teems with life. There is heartbreaking pathos too, particularly over the death of Nancy. She seems too good for the world she inhabits and does her best to help Oliver despite the personal cost to herself. In the end she is brutally murdered and it breaks our hearts, just as it broke the hearts of the

thousands of people who wept bitterly when Dickens read the passage to them on his tours.

DAVID COPPERFIELD

Popular appeal

David Copperfield began in serialisation in 1849. From that time it became a firm favourite among the public. They might have agreed with Dickens when he wrote, 18 years after first publication began:

> Of all my books, I like this the best. It will easily be believed that I am a fond parent to every child of my fancy, and that no-one can ever love that family as dearly as I love them. But, like many fond parents, I have in my heart of hearts, a favourite child.

> Preface to the 1867 edition of *David Copperfield*

Tolstoy went so far as to say: 'If you sift the world's prose literature Dickens will remain; sift Dickens, *David Copperfield* will remain; sift *David Copperfield*, the storm at sea will remain.' (quoted in *The Dickensian*, 45, 1949, p. 144).

This popularity probably stems from a sense of identification the reader has with David himself and the strong sense of childhood and self which permeate the novel. The plot is quite complex but it unrolls with an easy grace and we get the sense of Dickens enjoying himself.

Despite popular appeal, the novel largely failed to capture critical attention in the mid-twentieth century and was eclipsed by such works as *Hard Times* and *Bleak House.* Attention did not pick up again until the 1970s, when the new critical theorists began to take notice (See Modern critical approaches, p. 62).

Autobiography or fiction?

David Copperfield was regarded by Dickens and later critics as being close to his own autobiographical experiences. It would be a mistake to see it as pure autobiography, or perhaps even as autobiography at all, for all the events are fictionalised. We may see a resemblance to Dickens' father in Mr Micawber, hints of his childhood humiliations in the blacking factory (David at Murdstone and Grinby's), and the sense of a poor boy making good and becoming a writer, but this does not make it **autobiography**.

The novel is a **Bildungsroman**. Taken at face level, this describes *David Copperfield* perfectly and sets it in a literary line stretching back to Weiland's *Agathon* in 1756. The growing interest in this literary form made it a natural vehicle for Dickens to explore his subject.

KEYWORDS

Autobiography From the Greek 'auto' – self, 'bio' – life, 'graphy' – writing. The writing of one's life story.

Bildungsroman A form first developed in Germany. A novel chronicling the 'education' of the hero in the school of hard knocks. The main character is usually inexperienced, innocent and well meaning.

Disciplined and undisciplined hearts

Traditional judgement has it that *David Copperfield* is a novel in which there is a pattern of opposition between those lacking in self-control (Steerforth, Micawber, Mrs Strong, Emily) and David who eventually learns how to take control of his life. The argument springs from the notion of the undisciplined heart, taken from the words spoken by Mrs Strong who, when explaining her past life to Dr Strong, talks of 'the first mistaken principle of an undisciplined heart', and this has been taken by traditional critics as being central to Dickens' purpose. One of the few critics to take an interest in *David Copperfield* in the 1950s, Gwendolyn B. Needham, ('Nineteenth Century Fiction', article reprinted in the Norton edition of *David Copperfield* (1990), pp794–805) takes this view and argues that David's journey is precisely that – the undisciplined, weak young man slowly coming to realise the value of taking responsibility for his actions and developing a disciplined heart.

Barbara Hardy (*The Moral Art of Dickens*, Athlone Press (1970)) took this further and argued that essentially, *David Copperfield* is a moral tale with a 'clear graph' of his progress to fulfilment. Simply put, she argued that the novel fails because it lacks the moral subtleties that we should expect of great novelists. Hardy's criticisms stem from the liberal traditionalist

The Micawbers wait.

stance that a successful literary text has to represent this kind of moral statement. The author can thus be judged to have failed or succeeded by the extent to which the 'moral' has been aesthetically and successfully presented. However, this notion of a binary opposition between the disciplined and undisciplined heart is not enough to explain the novel. Modern criticism also deals with this opposition but (as you might expect) starts to see it as more complex than a mere binary opposition.

Sex, gender and the family

Once Dickens as moralist has been let off the hook, we can examine the text for what it tells us about Victorian attitudes to male/female relationships, sexuality, the family and the political and social structure of the time. Commenting on an essay by Cris Vanden Bossche, 'Cookery, not Rookery: Family and Class in David Copperfield', John Peck tells us that:

The result [of the arguments in the essay] is that *David Copperfield*, a novel that has struck many as one of Dickens' least complicated, emerges as a multi-layered work, centrally engaged in all the questions the Victorians were asking about themselves and about society, about self, about gender roles, indeed about the whole political structure of their world.

David Copperfield and Hard Times, (ed) John Peck, Macmillan, (1995),
Introduction, p. 11

There is much to explore beyond the simple narrative. There are issues of identity and self muddled up with sexuality and gender. For example, what are we to make of David's strong (seemingly homoerotic) attachment to Steerforth? Likewise, what should we make of the exploration of prostitution, the close relationship between the Murdstone siblings, and the various conflicting images of marriage in the novel? Modern criticism has much to say on the matter whether it be New Historicism, Feminism or the Psychoanalytics. (Chapter 8 Modern Critical Approaches.)

Identity through writing

David Copperfield is also a **Künstlerroman**, a novel about the education of an artist and so also, in this case, is about becoming a writer and the process of writing itself. The first

KEYWORD

Künstlerroman A novel about the education of an artist.

sentence indicates that we are to explore the notion of writing and the popular notion of the hero: 'Whether I shall turn out to be the hero of my own life, or whether that station will be held by anybody else, these pages must show.' David himself becomes a well-known writer and there are several other references to writing: Dr Strong is compiling a dictionary (he has only got to 'D' so far) and Mr Dick is writing a memorial (but is constantly hindered by the head of Charles the Martyr). These are all ways of fixing a life and, in the case of the last two examples, show how unsatisfactory writing can be as a means of constructing the present or the past.

The Shadows

Dickens on several occasions uses the word 'shadowy', and David himself mentions 'the shadows which I shall now dismiss', in the last line of the book. These references remind us of several things: the shadowy, dangerous nature of the world we grow up in, the shadowy insubstantial nature of memory and the shadowy nature of the picture conjured up by words on a page. Life is insubstantial and Dickens leaves us with this thought at the end of his tale, even as he paints a picture of domestic bliss with Agnes.

David Copperfield is a complex mix of highly entertaining characters, strong themes and situations. It sets off in autobiographical mode but interestingly places David in a higher social station than Dickens himself at the start of his life and so David does not have so far to travel to reach his true social station. The novel ends peacefully and with an air of contentment, something Dickens himself could only speculate about in his own life and something that speaks more of fiction than autobiography.

HARD TIMES

A novel rediscovered

Hard Times is the novel selected by F.R. Leavis, the notable academic, as Dickens' greatest achievement. Prior to that it had been one of the less popular novels and not one that would have sprung to the mind of the average reader. It began in serialisation in 1854, appearing weekly on the front page of *Household Words*. It is the shortest of the novels and seemingly one of the least complex, dealing with a single main theme and having no complicated subplots. It centres around the families of Gradgrind and Bounderby, is set (atypically for Dickens) in the north of England, and focuses on the effects of the philosophical, social, industrial and financial ethos of the time.

Setting the scene

The setting for the novel is the choking, gasping, grasping Coketown:

> It was a town of machinery and tall chimneys, out of which interminable serpents of smoke trailed themselves for ever and ever, and never got uncoiled ... You saw nothing in Coketown but what was severely workful.
>
> *Hard Times*, Chapter 5

The streets are monotonously regular, the river is polluted, and the people are 'equally alike one another'. They perform similar menial tasks year in year out. They exist to keep the great machine of industry turning, working for the greater good, and ironically receive no 'good' whatsoever in return.

In this bleak, monochrome landscape unfolds a human tale. Not only are Gradgrind and Bounderby defeated, but certain colourful characters save the day, including Sissy Jupe who looks after her adoptive family as best she can; and Mr Sleary whose intervention helps to ameliorate the disaster of Tom's criminal act.

Utilitarianism and the Poor Law

The major concern of Dickens was the social paradigm based on the philosophy of **Utilitarianism**. The intention of the Utilitarians was to bring about benign change but the paradoxical result of their efforts was to bring about misery, most notably seen in the cruel unfeeling nature of the 1834 Poor Laws. Factory owners could see many advantages in Utilitarianism, justifying their unashamed exploitation of their employees against their own wealth and the benefit brought to society by mass production. These inequities annoyed Dickens intensely but he also reacted strongly to Bentham's opposition to imaginative literature. Two of Bentham's aphorisms were:

KEYWORD

Utilitarianism A political, economic and social doctrine which based all values on utility. Everything was to be valued on the principle of the greatest good for the greatest number of people. It is mainly ascribed to Jeremy Bentham and John Stuart Mill, but was based upon philosophies developed in the eighteenth century as a means of coping with population growth and the influx of large numbers of people into the towns.

'Quality of pleasure being equal, push-pin is as good as poetry', and 'All poetry is misrepresentation'. *Hard Times* is an obvious and sharp response to these concepts. Dickens knew the power of words and, just as in *Oliver Twist*, set out to defeat the forces of barbarism and to prove his point by using imaginative fiction.

In *Hard Times*, Utilitarianism is championed by Thomas Gradgrind and the tone of the novel is set in the first three chapters where we meet him in the schoolroom demonstrating his philosophy. In a marvellous comic scene we are also introduced to some of the other main characters: Sissy Jupe, Bitzer, Louisa and Tom. They are to become the products of a universal school system (already being implemented as Dickens wrote) heavily dependent on the didactic and eschewing the imaginative. When Gradgrind tells Mr M'Choakumchild, the new teacher fresh out of training college (what a gloriously ironic name!), that what he wants is 'Facts', he is simply representing the new system of state education being built at that time.

Fact or Fancy?

It is clear to the reader early on, when Gradgrind finds his young son and daughter peering through the fence at Sleary's circus, that his philosophy will not be able to fill their whole lives and this introduces the other side of the coin to us – the world of the imagination. Sleary represents one of Dickens' key principles of writing, that 'people must be amuthed', and it is through Sleary that Dickens demonstrates the power of Fancy over Fact (see chapter on Themes, p. 22). In the process, Gradgrind finds out the hard way the terrible effect his teaching has had upon his children and his marriage. Gradgrind's unyielding philosophy and the patriarchy attendant upon it largely destroys his family.

Gradgrind's friend, the industrialist Bounderby (another glorious name), simply uses Utilitarianism for his own ends and Dickens employs him to show how greed and the motif of the self-made man are hollow. He exposes him eventually as the hypocrite that he is, and lays the lie that the good of one is the good of all in a compassionate society.

Should the child be indulged in Fact or Fancy?

Dickens and unionism

Industrial issues are examined through Stephen Blackpool, the representative of the individual in the system. Blackpool suffers a miserable life as a Coketown 'hand', is trapped in a marriage which precludes his finding fulfilment with Rachael, is victimised by the other factory hands and falls foul of the union leader Slackridge, before being dismissed ignominiously. In Dickens' eyes he falls between the twin evils of the self-interested employer and the fanatical demagoguery of Slackridge. Today, Dickens' portrait of unionism tends to jar but the novel is about what happens when things are taken to extremes, and about how little opportunity individual have to improve their lot under such a system. Dickens supported the rights of workers to good housing and sanitation and access to a proper education, but baulked at any idea of socialism.

George Orwell, in a generally supportive account of Dickens, criticises him for continually making moral attacks on all aspects of society, law, government, and education but never suggesting what should be done to improve them. Nowhere is this more obvious than in *Hard Times* where both laissez-faire capitalism and trade unionism are roundly condemned but no suggestion is made for improvement. Orwell believes the message is merely the platitudinous: 'If men would behave better the world would be decent' (Orwell, G., 'Charles Dickens' in *Inside the Whale and Other Essays*, Penguin (1940)).

Hope

Of course, if we take away the need for the novelist to supply answers, we can still enjoy the posing of the questions. When two opposing ideologies meet, there is bound to be friction. In Coketown, the parameters seem fixed and there is little opportunity for change. Bounderby, Bitzer and Tom all demonstrate this and Blackpool, in the tightest of corners, can only utter: 'T'is a muddle and that's aw.' They are victims of their education and environment. But there is hope for change and growth. Sissy Jupe overcomes her background and education, as does Louisa Gradgrind. Thomas Gradgrind himself, utterly defeated by his own philosophy, does recognise the consequences of his actions and makes great efforts to reform himself and redeem his family. (For more on the family, see Modern Critical Approaches).

Hard Times, as the title suggests, deals with conflict and misfortune but it is not a gloomy novel. There is plenty to raise the spirit including Louisa's resistance to the temptations of adultery; the humiliation of Mrs Sparsit and Bounderby; and various moments of high comedy including the early schoolroom scene and Mrs Sparsit's determination to shame Louisa – heightened by the delicious fact that we know what Mrs Sparsit does not.

Hard Times as fairy tale

Hard Times is not a realistic novel. Dickens was a great man of the theatre and this novel seems to be set in the harsh glare of limelight with its concomitant dark shadows. The often grotesque caricatures are familiar to connoisseurs of satire (and its related genre, horror), who know the powerful effects of exaggeration. The readers of *Punch* magazine in its heyday, followers of Ralph Steadman and viewers of the 1990s TV satire *Spitting Image* will all recognise the technique. Many commentators refer to the novel as fairy tale. Peter Ackroyd, for example, sees it as a 'fairy story of the industrial age' (*Introduction to the Works of Charles Dickens*, Mandarin (1991), p. 131). Steven Connor gets to the heart of the matter when he says:

> It is for this reason that fairy tale is so important in *Hard Times* as in many other Dickens novels; fairy tale is precisely that form of narrative which permits imaginative exceeding of the limits of the real world.

'Deconstructing Dickens: Hard Times' in *David Copperfield and Hard Times*, Peck, J. (ed), Macmillan (1995)

Pip meets Miss Havisham and Estella.

Hard Times is exactly at the nub of the debate between reality (Fact) and the imagination (Fancy). It is fitting that Dickens should forward the cause of Fancy by using one of its major forms to present his views.

GREAT EXPECTATIONS

Great Expectations was published in weekly serialisation in 1860. It is one of the most entertaining and satisfying of all Dickens' novels. Drama and suspense begin in the very first chapter and are maintained and built throughout. The dénouement is cleverly designed to frustrate the reader's expectations and eventually supplies an affirmative ending. It is also another example of a Bildungsroman.

Innocence and experience

The story revolves around the notion of innocence corrupted, a reworking of Blake's theme in *Songs of Innocence and Experience*. Initially Pip lives in a Garden of Eden, a rustic idyll spoilt only by the stern discipline and violence of Mrs Joe. Through external events (meeting Miss Havisham and the receiving of the bequest), and through his sense of guilt and of being tainted by criminality, he leaves that world to inhabit another, more refined, less 'common' and 'coarse'. As Pip sets off on his new life, this break with Paradise is made clear:

> We changed again, and yet again, and it was now too late and too far to go back, and I went on. And the mists had all solemnly risen now, and the world lay spread before me.
>
> Great Expectation, Book 1, Chapter 19

Pip is leaving behind his childhood. Dickens conveys the idea that childhood is rather innocent despite Mrs Gargery's brutal treatment. It is Pip's relationship with Joe which makes it innocent. Joe shares similarities with Mr Dick in *David Copperfield*. Both are male adult children whose benign presence signifies wisdom through innocence. This is in direct contrast to people like Jaggers in *Great Expectations*, who is so steeped in sordidness and dirt that he cannot wash it from his hands or like Skimpole in *Bleak House* where innocence is seen as a self-centred, parasitic and manipulative.

Early in the novel Pip becomes an innocent drawn into a criminal world, similar to Oliver in *Oliver Twist*. He is forced to steal for Magwitch and later is again obliged to harbour and abet him, a convicted felon and deportee.

Pip's journey is one which has him leaving his 'real' world, with its set order and with his place securely within it, and travelling far up a social scale to which he aspires and largely fails to understand. He is moved inexorably away from his roots towards a more sophisticated life predicated on money and social standing. As this occurs, he finds himself dislocated from his true feelings and insensible to the needs and aspirations of the world of Joe and Biddy. There are echoes here of Dickens' own dilemma: that of becoming famous and rich through his writings about social issues and thus becoming more and more removed from his sources of inspiration.

F.R. Leavis felt that:

> Dickens' preoccupations in *Great Expectations* are with the fundamental realities of society and focus on two questions: 'How was it that a sense of *guilt* was implanted in every child, and with what consequences? And what part does *class* play in the development of such a member of that society?

(op cit p. 288).

The making of a gentleman

Certainly one of the main pervading themes in *Great Expectations* is the question of what it is that makes someone a gentleman. Pip, in his quest to leave the rough life of the rural village, constructs a vision of his social standing which entails his climbing the social ladder (a familiar theme) with aspirations of becoming a gentleman and marrying Estella. At all times we see him singularly failing to acquire the true trappings of a gentlemen: he may learn to eat without putting his knife in his mouth but he almost always fails to deal with his friends in gentlemanly ways. (For a fascinating account of this topic see Robin Gilmour, 'Pip and the

Victorian Gentleman' in *Great Expectations*, Sell, D. (ed.), Macmillan (1994).)

Town versus country

One of the plot's main axes is that of the town–country dichotomy. The novel explores the romantic notions of lively urban sophistication versus the rural idyll. Yet neither is as ideal as it sounds. Underneath the perceived sophistication and excitement of town life lies an underworld of criminality and squalor. The sound moral economy of rural life with its strong work relationships, sense of community and cleanliness, is actually limiting and tedious:

> The country boy is bowled over by the city. The tired urbanite dreams of the country. But although the urbanite's fantasies may be mere wish fulfilment, they are terribly strong, and Dickens himself is worried that urbanisation may involve the loss of something profoundly important.
>
> Sell, D., *Great Expectations*, Macmillan (1994), Introduction, p 10

Having Pip go back and forth between the two states emphasises the differences between them just as Wemmick's town life and 'country' life contrast so vividly. Wemmick is one character who seems to be able to manage both worlds and exploit the benefits of both.

Women and expectations

Women play a very important role in Pip's progress: the dead mother, the cruel sister, the 'good' biddable Biddy, the eccentric manipulative Miss Havisham, and the ice-maiden Estella being the most obvious and influential. Much literary criticism of the late twentieth century has focused upon this. (See Chapter 8, Modern Critical Approaches.)

Realism and symbolism

As we have seen, Dickens' critics often attacked him for his lack of realism. In *Great Expectations*, Leavis (ibid p. 288) argues that Dickens managed to reconcile realism and symbolism so that:

In this novel, we move without protest, uneasiness even, from the 'real' world of everyday experience into the non-rational life of the guilty conscience or spiritual experience.

Leavis, *Great Expectations*, ibid, p. 288

To some extent this is an effect of the writing. The first person mature narrator, reflecting on his life but only allowing a view of the story as it unfolds chronologically, allows us to experience the tale through the young narrator's eyes and yet at the same time enables us to appreciate the ironies of knowing where he is misguided in thought and deed. To this extent, the novel reflects the experience of its readers who feel that *Great Expectations* somehow speaks to their own experience because they know that the novel reflects how life, and growing up, are an improvised process.

＊＊＊＊SUMMARY＊＊＊＊

- Oliver Twist is a novel of social conscience. Conceived as a critique of the 1834 Poor Laws it grew into one of Dickens' best loved works.

- Traditionally *David Copperfield* is seen as a story showing the triumph of self-control over an 'undisciplined heart'. Modern critical approaches don't accept this simple binary opposition.

- In *Hard Times* Dickens turns his attention to education, particularly to satirise the Utilitarian insistence on Fact over Fancy.

- *Great Expectations* is a novel concerning the corruption of innocence and the construction of the self.

Major works II: *Bleak House*

THE NOVEL AS A WHOLE

For the modern reader the first impression of *Bleak House* must surely be its length. In most editions it extends to over 950 pages of text. The intention of this chapter is to provide a way into the novel as a whole and introduce readers to the main themes and ideas that Dickens explores in this important work.

THE OPENING OF BLEAK HOUSE

The opening of the novel is justly a famous piece of writing but it is also, for the modern reader, a confusing one. Instead of taking us straight into the story, Dickens begins a highly descriptive account of a London covered in fog, soot and water. It is useful to ask ourselves what is going on here? What is the effect of this writing? What sort of expectations are being set up in us as readers of this text?

One effect of the opening can be seen in terms of obfuscation: everything is either covered in mud or soot or is hidden from view by fog. The language and the contemporary references to things like 'cabooses', 'collier brigs', 'gunwales' and 'the yards' add to the modern reader's confusion. Everything is difficult to see and totally chaotic. Dogs and horses seem to be indistinguishable; people are covered in mud and are slipping and sliding into each other; and tempers, not surprisingly, are beginning to fray. This is extenuated in the second paragraph in which fog would seem to have permeated every aspect of human endeavour.

Another effect is to locate the story very definitely in London. The city is, after all, given prime position, having an opening sentence all to itself. The Lord Chancellor and the legal system would also seem to have a significant role to play as we are led directly from the city itself into Lincoln's Inn and the Lord Chancellor.

The third effect of this opening is created by the language itself. The sentences are often short and direct, heightened by the use of semi-colons. Yet the language is anything but direct, as evidenced by the sudden appearance of the Megalosaurus in a succession of highly evocative similes. The means of expression is highly figurative. The smoke descends in a 'soft black drizzle', the comparison is with snowflakes that have 'gone into mourning'. It is worthwhile trying to read the opening paragraphs aloud or listening to a recording to get some sense of the sound of the language. For example, what effect is created by repetition of the word 'fog' at the beginning of sentences or clauses in the second paragraph?

Another obvious effect is quite simply that there is an awful lot of fog! And it is everywhere. There can be no escape from its murky, blinding effects. At another less literal level we can see the fog as the central symbol within the novel. Fog, like the law of Chancery, is both all pervasive and effectively blocks any form of human progress. The ships on the river, the pensioners at Greenwich and the people on the bridges are all impeded by the dark murky density of the fog. Likewise the law. There can be no progress for any of the characters whose destiny lies bound up in the laws of Chancery.

The opening of the book places these two forces, law and fog, side by side and so establishes both a theme and a metaphor for the whole novel.

A COMPLEX PLOT

The plot of *Bleak House* is a complex one that revolves around two quite distinct stories. These seem to be interrelated as they involve largely the same characters, although in essence they remain separate stories with separate resolutions. The first thread concerns the seemingly interminable case of *Jarndyce v Jarndyce* and the unfathomable workings of the Court of Chancery. To this is linked the fate of Richard Carstone, who along with his cousins, Ada Clare and John Jarndyce, is one of the three suitors in the case. The essence of the case is to establish exactly what proportion of the estate each should inherit, although, as Dickens implies, the underlying purpose would seem to be the continued employment of legions of solicitors and barristers.

The second thread is the mystery of Esther Summerson's birth and her relationship to the beautiful and haughty Lady Dedlock. This second story is considerably more complex than the first and provides much of the suspense and intrigue within the novel.

The complexity is heightened because so many characters are involved either centrally or on the periphery with both stories and almost every character is in some way connected with every other character in the novel.

THE FABRIC OF RE-OCCURRENCE

Many key aspects of the novel (character, plot, place) are interlinked in a variety of quite complex ways. It will help when reading the novel to have some understanding of how this interlinking works. It is part of what J. Hillis Miller calls the 'complex fabric of re-occurrences' within the novel:

> Characters, scenes, themes and metaphors return in proliferating resemblances. Each character serves as an **emblem** of other similar characters. Each is to be understood in terms of his reference to others like him/her. The reader is invited to perform a constant interpretative dance or lateral movement of cross-reference as he makes his way through the text.
>
> Introduction to *Bleak House*, Penguin (1971) reproduced in Connor, S. (ed.), *Longman Critical Reader: Charles Dickens*, Longman (1996), p. 62

Synecdoche

For Miller, the first level at which this interconnectedness works is through a device called **synecdoche**

This is a device well suited to a novel that is so consciously social and political. It means that we can understand the characters both at a literal level and a level representative of a larger social group. We learn a certain amount about Tulkinghorn, the central lawyer in the novel. We learn that he is corrupt, devious,

KEYWORDS

Emblem Symbolic representation of a quality, action or type of person.

Synecdoche [sin-ek-dokay] A figure of speech in which a more inclusive term is used for a less inclusive one or vice versa. A part of something can stand for the whole, or the whole for a part.

manipulative, powerful and twofaced. Yet his characterisation also works at the level of synecdoche. In this sense he (and the other lawyers Vholes and Conversation Kenge) is seen as representing the whole fraternity of lawyers, particularly those involved in the Court of Chancery. What Dickens is saying here then is not just that these particular characters are corrupt, devious, manipulative, etc., but that the law as a whole and its representatives are similarly corrupt. The part here represents the whole very forcefully.

This same synecdochal correspondence can be seen throughout the novel. The Dedlocks are representative of a decayed and yet still powerful aristocracy; the Boodles, Doodles and Coodles are another glimpse into this representation. Similarly, and most powerfully, Jo represents a plague upon Victorian England, the street child.

Miller suggests the second level at which the interconnectedness works is through **metaphor**. One character is, again with much conscious deliberation, held up and compared with another. There are, for example, striking and most obviously deliberate similarities between Krook and the Lord Chancellor. Krook is even known as the Lord Chancellor:

KEYWORD

Metaphor A figure of speech where something is described by comparing it with something else sharing similar properties.

> 'My landlord, Krook,' said the little old lady, condescending to him from her lofty station as she presented him to us. 'He is called among the neighbours the Lord Chancellor. His shop is called the Court of Chancery. He is a very eccentric person. He is very odd. Oh, I assure you he is very odd!'
>
> *Bleak House*, Chapter 5

There are also similarities between Tulkinghorn, Conversation Kenge and Vholes. There are similarly resemblances between the various Chancery suitors: Richard, Miss Flite, Gridley and Tom Jarndyce, all of whom are in one way or another ruined by the inexorable slowness of the process of law. There are other, less obvious, duplications: the fate of Esther's doll (Chapter 3), Esther herself as a baby (revealed in various places throughout the novel)and the brickmaker's baby (Chapter 8) combine to create one strand. Another line of resemblances is demonstrated by the number of obviously bad parents there are in the novel, the Jellybys, the Dedlocks, the Pardiggles, the Smallweeds and, of course, the Lord Chancellor who stands in *loco parentis* to Ada and Richard.

It is useful when reading to think about how these episodes are similar and what connections are being suggested by these similarities. It is important also to notice the differences which can similarly be described. Krook is not the Lord Chancellor; Esther did not die, although her mother long believed she had. The lawyers can be marked by their differences as well as their similarities. Also notice the relationship between George Rouncewell and his mother which is more a case of a neglectful child than a neglectful parent. To understand why this is important we have to understand something about the way metaphors work as well as something about what Dickens achieves in using these metaphors.

HOW METAPHORS WORK

A metaphor takes two separate entities and finds ways in which they are similar. For example, a thrown ball flying through the air and a rocket. The ball can be said to 'rocket through the air', suggesting that it is moving very quickly. The effectiveness of the metaphor relies on the fact that there are similarities between the ball and the rocket but also on the fact that they are different. If we were to describe a rocket flying through the air by saying that it 'rocketed though the sky' then language, or at least meaningful language, begins to break down. Of course a rocket 'rockets through the sky': what else could it do? A metaphor, then, works by holding two entities together but also by insisting that they are different.

Metaphorical connections in Bleak House

The same principle applies to Dickens' use of these metaphorical connections between characters in *Bleak House*. Krook and the Lord Chancellor are similar, they share the same name for a start. They also share other characteristics. Krook cannot read. He can only read individual letters, he cannot put them together to make meaningful words and sentences. Similarly, the work of the Lord Chancellor is fragmented; the way in which cases are presented in the Court of Chancery means they can never be put together, never concluded. It is, of course, ironical that Krook also holds the one piece of evidence that would solve the Jarndyce *v* Jarndyce case but, of course, because he cannot read, he doesn't know he has it! Yet Krook and the Chancellor are also different. One is poor and powerless and the other rich and powerful. Krook is a rag and bone dealer, the Lord Chancellor, at a literal level at least, is most certainly not.

This way in which characters are compared but also defined by their dissimilarity is important in the novel: Esther survives her bad parenting, the brickmaker's baby does not. Esther is also from a different social class. She will survive her poor parenting, as she is after all the child of an aristocrat. By holding these two apart and comparing them Dickens can make a valuable social point. Bad parenting has its problems but when this is combined with poverty and deprivation then the consequences will be fatal.

DECAY AND NEGLECT

In *Bleak House* we can identify several of Dickens' pet themes: injustice, class inequality, arrested development and poverty, but without doubt the central theme of the novel is that of decay and neglect. What was once functional has now fallen into decay. This is most clearly explored in the descriptions of the workings of the Court of Chancery.

THE COURT OF CHANCERY

This was originally established by Richard II in the fourteenth century. It dealt with wills and trusts. As the case of Jarndyce *v* Jarndyce shows, by the nineteenth century the court was hopelessly inefficient. While a case was 'in Chancery' all the assets were frozen. Once a case was finally settled, a process that took a very long time, the first costs to be met were those of the lawyers and the court. The process was made even more bureaucratic by the fact that individuals could only be represented in the court by a barrister who in turn took his directions from a solicitor. The largely written evidence that was submitted to the court had, of course, in the days before the photocopier, to be copied laboriously by hand.

What had once been an effective way of dealing with disputed properties was now wholly corrupt, serving only to line the pockets of men such as Vholes and Tulkinghorn. Dickens vividly portrays the effects of this corruption in the character of Richard Carstone, a man whose vitality and energy is slowly sucked out of him as, unable to settle on any other profession, he devotes his life to resolving the case. Notice particularly here the character of Vholes and the reference to his vampire-like qualities, most obviously in Chapter 50 but with frequent subtle references elsewhere in the book.

Decay is explored in many other ways in the novel. It can be seen at work within the Smallweed family where the senility of the grandmother is matched by the physical frailty of the grandfather and matched, too, by the stunted intellectual growth of Young Smallweed of whom the narrator tells us:

Everything that Mr Smallweed's grandfather ever put away in his mind was a grub at first, and is a grub at last. In all his life he has never bred a single butterfly.

Bleak House, Chapter 21, p. 332

This vivid metaphor suggests a complete collapse of human progress, decay to the point of sterility. There is nothing about the younger Smallweed that can ever be said to grow. The theme of stagnation and decay is explored, too, in the Dedlock family with its genetic inheritance of gout, and in the family home of Mr and Mrs Jellyby where the children are neglected, blinded by the pursuit of philanthropy. Most graphically it is explored in the descriptions of Tom-all-Alone's and the fate of the poor who are compelled to live in its ruins.

INTERCONNECTEDNESS

If the theme of decay is central to the novel, it is Dickens' insistence on the interconnectedness of all aspects of society which makes this decay so chilling. Dickens was no socialist, and yet he understood that our lives are interconnected. James Brown puts it this way in his study of Dickens:

> The novel shatters the cosy fiction that respectable society can have no connection at all with the wretched, ragged inhabitants of an urban slum, such as Tom-all-alone's. It argues that we are all in this together, all members and groups necessarily connected as part of one total system.
>
> *Dickens: Novelist in the Market Place*, Macmillan (1982), p. 57

The inter-linking of characters and the parallels between the two stories ensure that the poverty, decay and disease which Dickens portrays so vividly in Tom-all-Alone's must inevitably extend its reach to all other worlds portrayed in the novel. Jo is used both as a literal carrier of this decay and also metaphorically to represent the spread of that decay into English society. As Brown points out, it is no accident that Jo is a crossing sweeper keeping the way clear for the passage of people and goods between one place and another. Thus Jo is the carrier of disease from the slum of Tom-all-Alone's into Bleak House, giving smallpox to first Charley and then Esther. He is also the link between Lady Dedlock and the paupers' graveyard, which is both the resting place for Esther's father and significantly the place where Lady Dedlock herself finally collapses.

The extreme poverty of Tom-all-Alone's was created by the Court of Chancery: that self-same corrupt process which was slowly sucking the lifeblood out of Carstone.

Dickens does not shrink from spelling out his themes when he deems it appropriate. As he moves from the comforts of Chesney Wold to the poverty of Tom-all-Alone's, his narrator asks:

> What connection can there be, between the place in Lincolnshire, the house in town, the Mercury in powder, and the whereabouts of Jo the outlaw with the broom?
>
> *Bleak House*, Chapter 16

The frequent references by John Jarndyce to the wind being in the east when he is disturbed will mean little to a modern audience. To a resident of London in the 1850s it meant the danger of disease spreading from the impoverished East End of London into the affluent and relatively disease-free West End. Dickens' warning to English society about the spread of corruption and decay is thus obvious.

Some of Dickens' fiercest rhetoric in the novel can be found in his descriptions of Tom-all-Alone's and the fate of Jo. In Chapter 46, the third-person narrator warns us that Tom will have his revenge:

> There is not an atom of Tom's slime, not a cubic inch of any pestilential gas in which he lives, not one obscenity or degradation about him, not an ignorance, not a wickedness, not a brutality of his committing but shall work its retribution, through every order of society, up to the proudest of the proud, and to the highest of the high. Verily, what with tainting, plundering and spoiling, Tom has his revenge.
>
> *Bleak House*, Chapter 46

Peter Ackroyd, in his biography of Dickens (1990), reminds us that such injustices were frequently taken up by Dickens in both his monthly magazine H*ousehold Words* and in speeches up and down the country.

TWO NARRATORS

In a bold experiment with form, Dickens makes use of two narrators. This provides us with a continually changing perspective of both the story itself and of the characters. The technique provides us with two quite different perspectives on events. There is the voice of the omniscient third-person narrator and the very different perspective of Esther Summerson who provides us with a personal and necessarily narrower view of events.

Esther is looking back at events after seven years. Her viewpoint offers a sense of stability: whatever else may have occurred, we know that Esther has survived.

The two narrators technique has attracted much critical attention in recent years. There is a considerable jump in tone and style as the reader crosses the threshold from one narrative voice to another. The feminist critic Virginia Blain makes the point that the omniscient third-person narrative voice is distinguishably and, given the time in which Dickens was writing, unavoidably male. There is thus a continual contrast of people, places and events:

> The inner perspective, the subjective viewpoint, the interest bounded by personal limits, these are the qualities typically, even archetypally, associated with the feminine principle, while objectivity, impersonality and largeness of vision all belong in the masculine realm.

> 'Double Vision and the Double Standard in *Bleak House*:
> A Feminist Perspective' (1985) reproduced in Tambling, J.,
> *New Casebooks: Bleak House,* Macmillan (1998), p. 67

It is useful to consider the difference between these two perspectives. For example, although the two narrators *appear* to tell the same story about the same characters this might not always in fact be the case. One might usefully also reflect on whether the voices are as distinguishably male and female as Blain suggests. Is the third person narrative always objective and impersonal? What about those moments when, for example, the injustices of Tom-all-Alone's are being presented to the reader? Is Esther always archetypically feminine? She would frequently seem to be the voice of reason, using deductive thinking, for example, to argue a point with Richard. Could it not be argued this is archetypically male?

Catherine Belsey suggests that the effect of having two narrators is the nemesis of a third: that of the reader who is continually putting together the clues offered by both Esther and the narrator and creating his or her own unwritten **discourse**. As the novel progresses what happens is the emergence of a synthesis.

> By this means, Bleak House constructs a reality which appears to be many-sided, too complex to be contained within a single point of view, but which is in fact so contained within the single and non-contradictory invisible discourse of the reader, a discourse which is confirmed and ratified as Esther and the ironic narrator come to share with the reader a 'recognition' of the true complexity of things.
>
> *Critical Practice*, Routledge (1980), p. 81

What Belsey is describing here would seem to be the process of reading, the way in which we as readers struggle to make sense of a complicated story, putting together the clues we are given by the text. In the case of *Bleak House* the presence of two separate discourses makes us work harder. It also, of course, reinforces the theme of interconnectedness, while presenting another of the novel's processes, that of deduction and detection.

BLEAK HOUSE AS DETECTIVE FICTION

Hillis Miller (op cit p. 35) suggests that deduction is an essential process in reading B*leak House*. The last quarter of *Bleak House* (from Chapter 50 onwards) is almost xclusively devoted to what we would see today as a piece of detective fiction. As such, the novel can claim to be one of the first examples

KEYWORD

Discourse Communication (usually but not exclusively written) that reflects and contains material seen as belonging to a particular ideology, often the dominant ideology, of the period.

of the genre, preceding Wilkie Collins' *The Moonstone* by some 15 years. Bucket, the detective with his curious powers, is also a forerunner of figures such as Sherlock Holmes, Father Brown, Hercules Poirot and Inspector Morse.

You will notice how the pace of the novel changes as the detection process begins. There is a move from the slow and considered pace of the early chapters where there is room for discursion and often much moralising, to a pace which seems stylistically to mirror the chase by Esther and Bucket through the English countryside.

✳ ✳ ✳ ✳ *SUMMARY* ✳ ✳ ✳ ✳

- The two plots of *Bleak House* are both complex and inter-related. Understanding the relationship between the two is central to understanding the novel as a whole.

- The central theme in the novel is that of decay caused by neglect.

- *Bleak House* can be seen as a novel about social and political injustice.

- It can also be seen as a novel about the human condition.

- Dickens saw our lives as being interconnected. One way in which this is shown in the novel is by the way in which the lives of rich and poor are interconnected. He deliberately and carefully emphasises these connections by a clever duplication of aspects of character and plot.

- *Bleak House* is also a 'whodunit' in which both we and Mr Bucket try to solve the mystery of Esther's birth and Tulkinghorn's death.

Modern Critical Approaches

REAPPRAISAL

In the early twentieth century Dickens' work, although remaining popular with his general readership, assumed less importance in the world of literature than it had in its Victorian heyday. A new set of writers and a new movement, Modernism, eclipsed him. The revival of Dickens in the academic world began with a reappraisal of his work by such writers as Edmund Wilson, I.A. Richards, William Empson and George Orwell. Theirs was the task of rescuing Dickens' reputation and giving him a more scholarly stature. Their reappraisal tended to be based around the elements of characterisation, plot, content, themes and style.

Gabrielle Pearson, in reviewing the revival of critical interest in the 1940s, talks of there having been a need to create a 'dark' Dickens to restore his reputation among academic critics. Pearson's analysis is to be found in an essay entitled 'Dickens: The Present Position' as a preface to an anthology of mid twentieth century criticism which she sums up as follows:

> These essays do not bring into prominence any startling new view of Dickens; perhaps in that respect they are typically mid-century and post revolutionary. What they do, however, is to pose questions about Dickens' mind. How philistine and how educated? What sort of a man is he – cruel or kind? These questions, though they do not intrude, nonetheless continually pose themselves just under the surface.

> *Dickens and the Twentieth Century*, Gross, J. and Pearson, G. (eds), Routledge (1963)

So by the mid-twentieth century, the debate had begun to move away from Dickens the popular, towards Dickens the man – the man with a history and a psychology. A man of his time. He was beginning to fall under the magnifying glass of historical perspective and psychoanalysis.

Pearson (writing in the early 1960s) points the way that the critical tide was flowing by stating that:

> Certainly most critics readily accept that even Dickens' more mature achievements are flawed by irrelevant material, conflicts of convention and passages of purely functional and uninspired bridging. What one notices, however, is the increased readiness to acknowledge the flaws without being paralysed by them.

ibid, p. xxii

Thus we see the way opening for the next re-evaluation of Dickens, at the hands of various schools of criticism. These radically affected the way we view Dickens.

Since then there has been a considerable rise in the amount of academic and critical interest shown in Dickens. We only have to look at the place he now occupies in university syllabuses as well as the number of critical studies published in recent years. What will be quickly apparent to anyone reading this criticism is the diverse range of approaches it represents. There seem to be so many different, often contradictory, views of Dickens both as a writer and as a man that readers may well be baffled in their search for meaning. This elusiveness is something that seems to be inherent in the Dickens' legend. Dickens is, after all, a man whose writing and personal life are full of contradictions.

DIVERSITY OF APPROACHES

This diversity of viewpoints is something that the most recent critical approaches would see as a strength rather than a weakness. Literary theory seems now to have abandoned its search for the meaning of a text, so favoured by the traditional approach to literature, and is prepared to content itself with multiple meanings, meanings that, for example, can only be seen in the context of their position within a particular ideological framework.

MEANING AND DEATH OF THE AUTHOR

Roland Barthes posed the following question: How can a text be said to have a meaning if words have different associations and nuances for each reader? We each have a different impression and experience of the word 'garden'. The garden you see in your head will be different to someone else's. If this is true then there can be said to be no reliable meanings in the text, and so, the text can be said to have no meaning. At this point the role of the author as communicator of a 'meaning' is obsolete and so Barthes proclaimed the death of the author.

The liberal-humanist approach essentially rested upon a close analytical reading of the text itself, tending to disregard what might lie beyond the words and to discount factors such as social background, political change, gender and historical process. The comfortable and commanding position achieved by this approach was blown away by the emergence of what is now termed simply 'theory'.

Theory

Theory is the term used to refer to the diverse and often opposed range of different critical theories which emerged after the dominance of the traditional approaches had been overturned in the 1970s and 80s. It is no exaggeration to describe this change as a revolution, or more accurately as a series of revolutions, the effect of which was to change the way we look at literature completely. These revolutionary movements were many and various and included among them **structuralism** and **post-structuralism**, **Marxism**, **gay/lesbianism**, **feminism**, and an application of psychoanalysis to literature. Interestingly this was also the period that saw a resurrection in the position of Dickens in academic circles. The renewed interest established by the likes of F. R. Leavis and Edmund Wilson in the 1940s and 50s was picked up by the other critics such as J. Hillis Miller and Terry Eagleton in the 1980s and 90s. Yet more interest in his work has been generated by a turn towards the emergence of two new forms of criticism, New Historicism in the USA and its more Marxist cousin **Cultural Materialism** in Britain. There are many very good introductions to these theoretical approaches and some guidance is given in the suggested reading list at the end of this book.

We would like now to introduce you to two specific approaches to Dickens, the feminist approach and New Historicism, and consider how these approaches have changed the way we think about Dickens.

THE NEW HISTORICIST PERSPECTIVE

New Historicism takes its origins largely from the work of the French philosopher Michael Foucault and concerns itself with a reappraisal of the past and of what we mean by history. The traditional historical viewpoint tended to see the past as contained within a single story, a tale that could be told with endless certainty. New Historicism has argued against any notion of historic certainty. We cannot simply encapsulate the past within a single narrative; the past, like the present, is far more complex than this. We also need to recognise that we can only see history from within our own culture, from within the system of values,

KEYWORDS

Post-structuralism An often rather loose term which refers to the process of deconstructing the text.

Marxist criticism Approach to literature which insists that ideology (particularly social class) has a major influence on both what is written and what is read.

Gay/lesbianism In this approach to literature sexual orientation is taken as a key category of analysis and understanding.

Cultural Materialism A politicised version of New Historicism which stresses the historical, cultural and political circumstances in which a text was produced.

Ideology A system of ideas or representations that dominates the conscious, and often unconscious, minds of groups and individuals.

attitudes and belief which so permeate our culture as to make them almost invisible, that is to say, in simple terms at least, from within our own **ideology**.

In effect, this means that we cannot take a text such as *Hard Times* and assume that it portrays an accurate picture of the industrial Midlands in the mid-1800s. It is more accurate to say that it presents only one viewpoint and one that will undoubtedly be heavily influenced by both the belief systems of the author and the culture from within which he writes. New Historicism also stresses that we too can never be objective; we can only see the past from within the framework of our own ideology.

HAPPY FAMILIES

Catherine Gallagher's study *The Industrial Reformation of English Fiction* (Chicago (1985)) can be seen as an example of new historicist criticism. It combines a close reading of the text with an interest in establishing the ideological framework of the novels. To achieve this she looks at a range of texts by Dickens, Gaskell, Eliot and others to look at the similarities between social changes in the nineteenth century and changes in literary form. *Hard Times*, like Gaskell's *North and South*, she characterises as a novel that attempts to tackle the problems of social disharmony by proposing that society takes as its model the co-operative behaviour epitomised in the private life of the family. Her close textual analysis of *Hard Times* allows her to trace this argument particularly in the opening chapters of the novel. The comparison between the public and private spheres is achieved, Gallagher argues, by means of a complex metaphor, constructed around the idea of social paternalism, that is established in the opening chapters of the novel. In part this is shown by the way in which the worlds of Gradgrind's school and his home are juxtaposed to invite comparison. If this were not enough, Dickens' narrator asks somewhat pointedly:

> Is it possible, I wonder, that there was any analogy between the case of the Coketown population and the case of the little Gradgrinds?
>
> *Hard Times*, Chapter 5

Gallagher believes that the first half of the novel attempts to provide an affirmative answer to this question. Think, for example, of the very conscious parallels in the relationship between Stephen, the factory worker, and Mr Bounderby, his employer on the one hand, and Louisa and her father on the other. These are very deliberately compared in the interview in Chapter 11 between Bounderby and Stephen and the interview in Chapter 15 between Louisa and her father.

Ultimately, though, Gallagher argues that the social paternalism model breaks down simply because it cannot and does not work. The idea that society can be reformed by adopting the values inherent in the family is also shown to be untenable in the novel itself as untenable. The Gradgrind family itself is always seen by the reader as dysfunctional; it has to be reformed before it can become a model of harmony and security and thus provide a proper paradigm for social relationships. It can only achieve harmony by removing itself into a position of social isolation. And here lies the problem. Interestingly, like *North and South*, the novel resolves itself by a retreat from the public realm. Thus it begins by advocating an integration of the public and the private and then resolves itself by insisting that the two must remain separate.

This is only a small sample of Gallagher's very rich text. It shows one way in which New Historicism examines the relationship between the political, the historical and the cultural. Gallagher shows that Dickens, by choosing this particular ending for his novel, demonstrates the instability of the relationships between the two realms of public and private in mid-century Victorian England. In this way *Hard Times* can be seen as a discourse that both reflects and interacts with the belief systems of the period.

UNHAPPY FAMILIES

Catherine Waters in her feminist/new historicist study *Dickens and the Politics of the Family* (CUP (1997) shows how the portrayal of both functional and dysfunctional families in Dickens' novels supports the Victorian middle class view of the centrality of the family and also of the **hegemonic** in the function of Dickens' novels. Dickens was a celebrated advocate of the family and yet

KEYWORD

Hegemony Concept developed by the Italian Marxist Gramsci to show the way in which a dominant power by manipulation, insisting that its own set of beliefs is taken as the norm and therefore not questioned. The role of the media and literature are seen as central to this process.

paradoxically, as we have seen, the ideal is established by means of the failures of other fictional families. These failures (and there are many of them in the Dickens' oeuvre) illustrate for Waters the 'normalising function of middle-class domestic ideology in Dickens' fiction'. The centrality of the family in Dickens' novels emphasised the importance of the structure for Victorian society. One could argue that Dickens provided a model of how a family should operate and how it should not.

THE FEMINIST PERSPECTIVE

Feminist criticism is a diverse and eclectic field of study. Its origins can be traced back to the women's movements of the 1960s and beyond. Early feminist criticism was polemical and combative, fighting against a dominant ideology that placed men hierarchically above women. In literature it fought against the negative constructions of women in fiction from housewife to whore, and later went on both to reclaim a female perspective in literature and redefine the literary canon to include many previously neglected female writers. More recent feminist criticism tends to concern itself with issues such as the relationship between gender, sexuality and power.

Dickens and women: The traditional view

The way Dickens portrays women has attracted much criticism. He has been accused of helping to reinforce the dominant Victorian ideology that kept women in subservient roles within the home and of treating with contempt any women who attempt to move out of these traditional roles. He has also been accused of being unable to create sexually mature female characters, preferring instead childlike, naïve and virginal male fantasies.

The Eccentric, the Imbecile and the Shrew

An example of such criticism can be found as early as 1898. George Gissing refers to Dickens' 'inability to represent any kind of woman save the eccentric, the imbecile and the shrew'.

It is a viewpoint pursued by many writers since who have lambasted Dickens for his restricted view of femininity. Orwell, for example, was highly critical of Dickens' inability to portray sexually mature women. John Carey, in his excellent study *The Violent Effigy*, makes the following comment:

> In the novels... an unbridgeable gap divides the pure young maids from the nagging married women, stupid, sexless, aggravating, their dynasty extending from Mrs Nickleby right through to Mrs Wilfer.
>
> Carey J, *The Violent Effigy*, Faber (1973) p. 158

The 'pure young maid' is viewed with concern by many commentators, particularly as she seems to appear always as a male fantasy figure in the Dickens' novel. She is usually portrayed as very young, innocent and sexually naïve. Esther Summerson in *Bleak House* is seen as the archetypal example of such a child/woman. Carey, like others, emphasises the childlike appearance of many of these heroines as well as their total dependency on more powerful men. Esther is totally dependent upon Mr Jarndyce, likewise Amy Dorrit (*Little Dorrit*), Rose Maylie (*Oliver Twist*) and Dora Spenlow (*David Copperfield*) are all shown as dependent upon their fathers and husbands.

It can be argued, however, that the criticism of Gissing, Orwell and Carey are unduly harsh. Certainly, it is not hard to find some of these female representations in the novels. Miss Havisham in *Great Expectations* might count as both an eccentric and a shrew; Mrs Sparsit (*Hard Times*) is most certainly a shrew as are Miss Murdstone (*David Copperfield*), Mrs Bumble (*Oliver Twist*) and the murderous Hortense in *Bleak House*. Imbecilic women would seem to be a sparser breed, often having only minor roles such as Gussie in *Bleak House*.

Yet it is important to ask whether it is really possible to be so categorical? Can we, for example, point to only a few 'types' and say that these are the only women we see in the novels?

Dickens as a writer of female discourses

While traditional criticism and early feminist commentary have tended to focus on the absence of strong female characters in Dickens' novels, more recent studies have attempted to resurrect Dickens and focus on his stronger, more positive portrayals of women. Louisa Gradgrind in *Hard Times* has long been seen as an exception to the Dickens' stereotype, with critics seeing her variously as passionate, forthright and rebellious. There has also recently been a focus on many of Dickens' other stronger women characters such as Lady Dedlock in *Bleak House* and also a tendency to see strength where other earlier studies have found weakness.

Jean Ferguson Carr's essay 'Dickens, Hard Times and Feminine Discourses' provides a completely different perspective on Dickens' work. It is also an example of a synthesis between the feminist and new historicist approaches. Rather than seeing Dickens as representative of the dominant patriarchy that regarded men and women as almost separate species and placed a higher value on men's business than on women's 'frivolities', she sees him as a writer who disrupted the social order. While not quite claiming him as a feminist she does suggest that at times he expresses a strong preference for feminine values and that nowhere is this more clearly expressed than in *Hard Times*.

It is important to note a different tone in Carr's essay than that adopted by the high priests of traditionalism. While not seeking controversy, the essay, like much modern criticism, is not frightened of making controversial comments. For example, the notion that Dickens was a writer of feminine discourses is in itself a very radical revision of his ideological position!

Dickens is seen as occupying an uneasy and often ambivalent position, taking a perspective which 'hovers at the edge of articulation', using a voice which seems empathic with women's position even to the extent that, like theirs at this time, it lacks articulation. *Hard Times* is seen as totally constrained by the Gradgrindian system, a system that allows only for the expression of facts and logic. Everything else is excluded to the extent that it cannot be articulated. Reason and logic seem to ring-fence the area of articulation in which the novel is spoken. Excluded from this world are imagination, 'Fancy' and any sense of a private domain that can express such fragile thoughts as feelings. The impossibility of expression is personified in the form of Mrs Gradgrind. While Carr agrees with most feminist readings of the text which see Mrs Gradgrind as an unsatisfactory figure, she sees this not as a fault in the writing but rather an example of Dickens' attempt to produce a feminine discourse. Mrs Gradgrind is seen as a translucent figure who continuously fails to produce for us a sense of herself. Even on her deathbed she can only hint that there is something unnameable and never fully graspable:

> But there is something – not an Ology at all – that your father has missed, or forgotten, Louisa. I don't know what it is. I have often sat with Sissy near me, and thought about it. I shall never get its name now.
>
> *Hard Times*, Book 2, Chapter 9

As such, Carr suggests, Mrs Gradgrind defines the boundaries of the Gradgrindian system. She stands just outside it, unable to express or even think what it is that the system is missing. It is left to Sissy Jupe and Sleary, the lisping circus master, to provide an oppositional view. Even then Carr suggests we get little of Sissy's view through her own lips; this is mostly provided by the narrator or men such as Harthouse and Gradgrind:

> Her effect is largely due to the novelty of her discourse, a novelty produced by her status as an outsider who does not understand the conventions of the system.
>
> 'Dickens, *Hard Times* and Feminine Discourses' (1989) reprinted in Peck, J. (ed.), *New Casebook: David Copperfield and Hard Times*, Macmillan (1995), p. 208

It is Sissy's lack of power, her lack of an appropriate language to express herself, that is given voice within the novel. Carr argues that she has no 'lore' or wisdom to pass onto Louisa other than simply being a working class child who has experiences outside the Gradgrindian system. There are, however, no means of expressing this different world view. The only view that can be expressed is a negative one, that what is contained within the Facts and reason of Gradgrind's world is somehow missing something, something that must remain unnameable. It is in the frustrated, even impossible, articulation of an alternative viewpoint that Carr identifies Dickens as writing as a woman. Like them, he can only hint that something is missing and in doing so subverts the conventions of his time.

Dickens writing as a woman

It is in *Bleak House*, of course, that Dickens literally writes as a woman. About half the novel is narrated by Esther Summerson. This is the only example in Dickens' work of his presenting material directly from a female perspective and so can be used to provide evidence of how Dickens imagined women saw their own roles.

Dickens writing as a woman.

A central question here for feminist critics is what sort of woman does Dickens portray in Esther? Some have seen her as a very poorly drawn figure, a mere male fantasy: subservient, domestic, youthful, innocent and wholly controlled by men. More recent studies have begun to find other aspects of her characterisation that argue against this view. Virginia Blain (in New Casebook: *Bleak House*, Tambling, J. (ed.), Macmillan (1998), pp. 65–86), for example, points out that this viewpoint can easily be turned on its head. Victorian middle class women in this period were expected to be totally subservient, their roles as wife and mother were totally prescribed for them, and any sense of individuality or independence would be regarded as a burden. What Dickens has created in Esther, she argues, is wholly representative: she is a woman of her time. Esther as a woman would have had no knowledge of, or access to, the legal, financial and political institutions of her time. Thus her insights into the workings of the Court of Chancery are extremely limited. She can only view them by the effects she sees on those around her, most dramatically on Richard whose slow suffocation she is powerless to stop. It can be argued that by showing Esther burdened by and entrapped within the constraints of womanhood, Dickens is merely highlighting the constraints of Victorian society.

Another view of Esther is provided by Suzanne Graver (in Ayres, B. *Dissenting Women in Dickens Novels*, Greenwood Press (1998)). She identifies two voices in Esther, the dominant one which is accepting and accommodating, and another that, while more muted, is also more inquiring, critical and discontented. Another feminist critic, Brenda Ayres, suggests this split raises interesting possibilities. Was Dickens insightful enough to create a woman who both experienced and expressed the fissure created by domestic ideology? Or is it rather a failure in the writing – the failure of a male writer to create a consistent female perspective?

Deviant women

The Victorian ideal of womanhood might be that depicted by Coventry Patmore in his poem 'Angel in the House'. This was a highly popular work both in England and America and was essentially a hymn to the subservience of women. There are plenty of examples of these in Dickens' novels, yet there are also many examples of deviant women who fail to live up to this high ideal. A gentle example of this would be Dora Spenlow, David Copperfield's 'child-wife'; pretty, charming but essentially empty-headed and a total failure as a housekeeper. But there are also many more initially less sympathetic deviant women depicted in the novels, for example Estella and Miss Havisham in *Great Expectations*.

Traditionally, Estella has not been viewed sympathetically. She is cold, beautiful and haughty and her role, to destroy the novel's hero, to break his heart, has not been seen as an attractive one. Michael Slater sees Estella as a 'beautiful monster'. Pip himself frequently despairs of ever finding salvation:

> Everything in our intercourse did give me pain. Whatever her tone with me happened to be, I could put no trust in it, and build no hope on it; and yet I went on against trust and against hope. Why repeat it a thousand times? So it always was.
>
> *Great Expectations*, Chapter 33

A feminist reading of Estella can point to other interpretations. Gail Houston (in Ayres, B. *op cit*) sees her as an archetype bred to be desired but to have no desire herself. Brenda Ayres sees her as a perfect product of Victorian ideology. Estella for her is the exact opposite of the 'Angel in the House'.

> Instead of submissive she is wilful and domineering. Instead of gentle, kind and tender she is calculating, malicious and hard. Instead of reserved she is acrimonious. Instead of internalising her suffering, as was expected of a good Victorian woman, she inflicts suffering on men.
>
> *Dissenting Women in Dickens' Novels*, Greenwood Press
> (1998), p. 90

GAPS AND FISSURES

One task which modern criticism undertakes is often to find the gaps in a text: to focus not on what is there, but rather on what is missing. One such obvious gap both in Dickens and almost all Victorian literature, for example, is any overt expression of sexuality. Lady Dedlock and Agnes, Oliver Twist's mother, both pay the ultimate penalty for their 'sin', but the sin itself is only expressed through the birth of their illegitimate children. Even prostitution is sanitised. Nancy in *Oliver Twist* is most obviously a prostitute. Dickens even tells us 'Nancy is a prostitute' in the preface to the 1846 edition, although this statement is absent from later editions. Yet, as we read the book, it becomes increasingly difficult to see her in this role. She 'ascends the spiritual ladder' that her suffering erects, as Michael Slater puts it in *Intelligent Person's Guide To Dickens* (1999) and becomes a heroine who sacrifices herself for a greater good.

In seeking out these gaps, feminist readings would seem to ask some very fundamental questions about what goes on within the Dickens' novel. On the surface of many novels there may appear to be a fine adherence to the notion that women should be passive, submissive, gentle and domestic, yet as we read, we are struck by how often we are left with a sense of something else, something which does not conform to this rigid social code. It is indeed as if within the woven fabric of the text there are gaps and fissures through which the conventionality would seem occasionally to tumble. One example of this can be seen if we ask: If Dickens is trying to portray something that is meant to be a reflection of his society why does he allow his reflections to fall apart so frequently? Louisa Gradgrind's devotion to her brother in *Hard Times* is surely shown to be ill-judged. Similarly Nancy's devotion to Bill Sikes might be noble but it is also fatal. On the surface the text may promote one sort of ideology but running under this are other ideologies that often work to subvert. Patriarchal rule is shown so often to represent a leadership lacking in either judgement or morality and sometimes both.

Both new historicist and feminist approaches provide us with new perspectives on the worlds created by Charles Dickens. They ask fresh questions and sometimes answer old questions in new ways. What is achieved is sometimes referred to as 'reading against the grain', that is offering a viewpoint which goes against the way it seems as if the reader's thoughts are being directed by the narrative. So, to use an earlier example, Mrs Gradgrind in *Hard Times* would seem in a raditional reading to be a weak, ineffective, somewhat pathetic figure, left behind by the powerful, if misguided, 'ologies' which drive her husband's brand of Utilitarianism. If we read against the grain, however, she can be seen as a representative of a viewpoint that values all those qualities that are necessarily excluded from the Gradgrind philosophy. That neither she nor other women in the narrative can effectively speak these qualities is symptomatic both of the position of women and the excluding power of a system of thought built exclusively on the rule of fact and logic.

✳ ✳ ✳ SUMMARY ✳ ✳ ✳ ✳

- There has been an enormous increase in the critical interest shown in Dickens since the mid -1960s.

- This has spawned a huge range of very diverse interpretations of his work.

- 'Traditional' literary analysis rested upon a close reading of the text and ignored extrinsic factors.

- Literary criticism has now itself splintered into many different and often competing factions.

- Catherine Gallagher suggests that in *Hard Times* a parallel is drawn between the family and the work-force. Ultimately the parallel fails.

- Catherine Waters points to the hegemonic functions of the novels, particularly in reinforcing the role of families.

- Modern feminist criticism looks at the relationship between gender, sexuality and power.

- Traditional criticism was very scathing in assessing Dickens portrayal of women.

- Modern criticism has tended to focus on the more positive characters, even suggesting that Dickens may have been sympathetic to the position of Victorian women.

Where Next?

READ HIS WORK

Read as much of Dickens as you can. The more you read the more the world of Dickens will open up to you. Apart from the novels already discussed there are plenty more: *Nicholas Nickleby, Little Dorrit, Pickwick Papers, Barnaby Rudge, Our Mutual Friend, The Old Curiosity Shop* and the unfinished *Mystery of Edwin Drood* being the most notable. If you want to read them in sequence you can use the chronology at the back of this book.

Then there are the numerous short stories and Christmas stories. The most famous of these being *A Christmas Carol, The Signalman* and the stories based around *Mr Humphrey's Clock.*

READ THE EXPERTS

Many modern editions of the works include excellent introductions by experts. They can be read with interest before or after reading a particular novel (or both).

When you have read the fiction you might find it interesting to take a look at the criticism. There are numerous critics and schools of critical thought, and you could take these further by reading from the original texts. There is no set order to read them in, but if you are of an orderly mind or like the chronological approach, you could start with the near contemporary reactions of George Gissing and Humphrey House, and then go on to examine the critics responsible for the Dickens' renaissance, such as Leavis and Orwell, before plunging into modern critical theory.

There are more and more books being published on Dickens. The following would be a good place to start:

* The *New Casebooks* series published by Macmillan collects together modern critical essays based around individual novels. Each contains a useful essay that introduces the reader to recent critical material.

* Peter Ackroyd's excellent biography simply called *Dickens* is published by Sinclair Stevenson.

* Michael Slater's *An Intelligent Person's Guide to Dickens* is a good introduction to some of the main themes in Dickens' work. His earlier book, *Dickens and Women,* is a fascinating exploration of the women in both Dickens' life and in the novels.

READ DICKENS' CONTEMPORARIES

Another approach is to read writers of a similar era, such as Trollope and Thackeray, George Eliot and Dickens' great friend, Wilkie Collins. They each have a different vision and set their novels in distinctly different fictional landscapes.

JOIN A DICKENS SOCIETY

The biggest society is the Dickens Fellowship, founded in 1902, in London (usually associated with the Dickens House Museum, Doughty Street). It has about 15 UK branches (one of which you might care to join), about 22 US branches and branches in New Zealand, Australia, France, India and Japan. The Fellowship's journal is *The Dickensian* (founded 1905), which comes out three times a year (currently edited by Professor Malcolm Andrew of the University of Kent). A Fellowship website is planned, which will contain details of branches and activities, including the annual Rochester and Broadstairs Dickens Festivals.

There is also the Dickens Society of America, with its journal *Dickens Quarterly. The Dickensian* tends to concentrate on scholarly, antiquarian, topographical and biographical work and the *Quarterly* on more purely critical studies and reviews.

The *Dickens Studies Annual* began publication in 1970 and is published in USA. This is a book-form annual collection of essays on Dickens and Victorian studies in general.

There are several websites dedicated to him and his works. Websites are always subject to change so you will have to use your web search engine intelligently to find out what you need. You could try: **http://members.tripod.com/~DickensFellowshipCD** as a starter.

Another big annual Dickens occasion – of a more scholarly kind – is the Dickens Universe. This is a big conference, hosted by University of California at Santa Cruz. The following website: **http://humwww.ucsc.edu/dickens/index.html**   contains   more information.

GO AND VISIT
There is much pleasure to be had in visiting places connected with Dickens, such as the places he lived (Gad's Hill, Dickens' House, Rochester, or his birth place in Portsmouth).

HAVE FUN
And, finally, there are the games to be played as you read. Taking topics such as Dickens and food, Dickens and clothes or the London of Dickens, you can set out to discover how important these subjects are to Dickens and how he tackles them.

Spotting well-known sayings can be interesting. 'Please Sir, I want some more' (*OT*), 'Barkis is willing' (*DC*), 'A horse: Graminivorous. Forty teeth, namely twenty-four grinders, four eye-teeth, and twelve incisive. Sheds coat in the spring; in marshy countries sheds the hoofs, too. Hoofs hard, but requiring to be shod with iron. Age known by marks in mouth' (*HT*).

Finally, there are the many colourful names of his characters to note and treasure, names which could become a poem in themselves: Mr Micawber, Steerfarth, Mrs Gamp, Wackford Squeers, Little Nell, Tiny Tim and so on. Dickens is a serious writer but he is also a lot of fun. We hope you continue to read and enjoy him for many years to come.

* * * *SUMMARY* * * *

- Read his work.

- Read the experts.

- Read his contemporaries.

- Join a society.

- Visit places of interest.

- Have fun.

GLOSSARY

Autobiography From the Greek 'auto' – self, 'bio' – life, 'graphy' – writing. The writing of one's life story.

Bildungsroman A form first developed in Germany. A novel chronicling the 'education' of the hero in the school of hard knocks. The main character is usually inexperienced, innocent and well meaning.

Cultural Materialism A politicised version of New Historicism based particularly on the work of Jonathan Dollimore and Alan Sinfield. It stresses the historical, cultural and political circumstances in which a text was produced.

Deconstructionism A way of reading 'against the grain' of a text to uncover what is below the surface

Discourse Communication (usually but not exclusively written) that reflects and contains material seen as belonging to a particular ideology, often the dominant ideology, of the period to which it belongs.

Emblem Symbolic representation of a quality, action or type of person.

Fancy A term, now much derided, used by Dickens to refer to the creative imagination.

Feminism The study of gender politics from a female perspective.

Gay/lesbianism In this approach to literature sexual orientation is taken as a key category of analysis and understanding. In Dickens, for example, it might look at the male-male and female-female relationships in opposition the male-female relationships in the text.

Hegemony Concept developed by the Italian Marxist Gramsci to show the way in which a dominant power maintains its supremacy by manipulation, insisting that its own set of beliefs is taken as the norm and therefore not questioned. The role of the media and literature are seen as central to this process.

Ideology A system of ideas or representations that dominates the conscious, and often unconscious, minds of groups and individuals

Künstlerroman A novel about the education of an artist.

Marxist Criticism Based on the political theories of Karl Marx and Friedrich Engels. A Marxist approach to literature which insists that ideology (particularly social class) has a major influence on both what is written and what is read.

Metaphor A figure of speech where something is described by comparing it with something else sharing similar properties.

New Historicism A theory which takes the view that there can be no historical certainty. The past can only be seen from within our own ideological present.

Parody Work in which themes and/or the style of a particular work/author are exaggerated or applied inappropriately for the purposes of ridicule.

Post-structuralism An often rather loose term which refers to the process of deconstructing the text. See also **Deconstructionism.**

Structuralism Intellectual movement originating in France in the 1950s in the work of Levi Straus and Roland Barthes. Stresses that things cannot be understood in isolation but need to be seen in a wider context.

Synecdoche [sin-ek-dokay] A figure of speech in which a part of something can stand for the whole, or the whole for a part.

Utilitarianism A political, economic and social doctrine which based all values on utility. Everything was to be valued on the principle of the greatest good for the greatest number of people.

Vivification Dickens' tendency to take one central characteristic and inflate it to the point where it takes over the whole character, e.g. Mrs Sparsit's Roman nose.

CHRONOLOGY OF MAJOR WORKS

1833 *A Dinner at Poplar Walk*, his first published piece in *The Monthly Magazine*

1834 Staff reporter on *Morning Chronicle*

1835 'Sketches of London' for *Evening Chronicle*

1836 Sketches by Boz published
   Pickwick Papers begun

1837 *Pickwick Papers* completed and issued in book form
   Oliver Twist begins in B*entley's Miscellany*

1838 *Nicholas Nickleby* begins in instalments
   Oliver Twist published in 3 volumes

1839 *Nicholas Nickleby* completed and published in book form

1840 *Master Humphrey's Clock* begins to appear weekly
   Old Curiosity Shop and *Barnaby Rudge* begin to appear in *Master Humphries Clock*

1841 *The Old Curiosity Shop* and *Barnaby Rudge* are published in book form

1843 *Martin Chuzzlewit* appears in monthly parts
   A Christmas Carol published

1844 *Martin Chuzzlewit* published in book form

1846 *Dombey and Son* appears in monthly parts

1848 *Dombey and Son* appears in book form

1849 First episode of *David Copperfield* appears in May

1850 *David Copperfield* published in book form
   Household Words first published with Dickens as editor

1852 Monthly serial publication of *Bleak House* begins
   First volume of A Child's History of England published

1853 *Bleak House* published in book form

1854 *Hard Times* appears weekly in *Household Words* and then published in book form

1855 *Little Dorrit* issued in monthly parts

1857 *Little Dorrit* published in book form

1858 Leaves *Household Words*
1859 Begins weekly magazine called *All the Year Round*
Buys out *Household Words*
A Tale of Two Cities serialised and published in book form
1860 *Great Expectations* in weekly parts in *All the Year Round*
1861 *Great Expectations* published in 3 volumes
1864 *Our Mutual Friend* in monthly instalments for Chapman and Hall
1865 *Our Mutual Friend* published in book form in 2 volumes
1869 Begins *Edwin Drood*
1870 *Edwin Drood* appears in six monthly parts, intended to be completed in 12 but left unfinished

FURTHER READING

There are hundreds of books about Dickens. Here are a few to get you started.

BIOGRAPHY
Ackroyd, P., *Dickens*, Sinclair-Stevenson (1990)

COLLECTIONS OF CRITICAL ESSAYS
Connor, S., (ed.), *Charles Dickens*, Longman (1996)
Lucas, J., *Charles Dickens The Major Novels*, Penguin (1992)
Peck, J., (ed.), *David Copperfield and Great Expectations*, Longman (1995)

RECENT STUDIES
Andrews, M., *Dickens and the Grown-Up Child*, Macmillan (1994)
Carey, J., *The Violent Effigy – A Study of Dickens' Imagination*, Faber (1973)
Slater, M., *An Intelligent Person's Guide to Dickens*, Duckworth (1999)

CRITICAL THEORY
Barry, P., *Beginning Theory*, Manchester University Press (1990)
Sedgewick, P. and Edgar, A., *Key Concepts in Cultural Theory*, Routledge (1999)

INDEX